Paul's Last Letter

Paul's Last Letter: A Commentary on the Second Epistle to Timothy

Mark Sweetnam

WIPF & STOCK · Eugene, Oregon

Wipf and Stock Publishers
199 W 8th Ave, Suite 3
Eugene, OR 97401

Paul's Last Letter
A Commentary on the Second Epistle to Timothy
By Sweetnam, Mark
Copyright © 2023 by Sweetnam, Mark All rights reserved.
Softcover ISBN-13: 979-8-3852-0896-8
Hardcover ISBN-13: 979-8-3852-0897-5
eBook ISBN-13: 979-8-3852-0898-2
Publication date 2/27/2024
Previously published by Scripture Teaching Library (STL), 2023

Preface

IN 2 TIMOTHY 2:2, Paul instructs Timothy to commit the things that he had heard from the apostle 'to faithful men, who shall be able to teach others also'. Looking over the pages of this book reminds me of many debts of gratitude that I owe, but chief among them is the incalculable amount that I owe to faithful men who have taught me the Scriptures and – no secondary benefit – how to study the Scriptures. Behind these teachers were the exercise and effort of overseers to arrange meetings, convene conferences, and to discharge their responsibility to 'feed the flock of God' (1 Pet. 5:2). The footnotes of this volume record the more readily identifiable debts, but only eternity will reveal the blessing of those who built with gold, silver, and precious stones.

1 Corinthians 3 may not recognise iron as a building material, but Proverbs 27:17 reminds us that 'Iron sharpens iron, and one man sharpens another' (ESV). I am grateful for good friends who have read and commented on drafts of this material, and who have helped me to sharpen and refine my thinking on these verses. As ever, I am deeply thankful for the fellowship and encouragement of the Christians who form the assembly in Rathmines, who have encountered some of the material contained herein at one time or another.

I am also grateful to Phil Coulson who, as the editor of *Believer's Magazine*, invited me to contribute the series articles that provided the genesis of the present volume and who bore with great equanimity not only the proliferating number of articles but my sometimes *laissez-faire* approach to wordcounts.

The articles that were the first draft of this book were, in part, written during the Covid-19 lockdown. Of the many challenges of that difficult period, one was of particular relevance – the inaccessibility of the Library of Trinity College Dublin, whose extraordinary resources I am normally able to plunder at will. In the crisis of Covid, the librarians there went above and beyond even their usual high standard of service to scholarship, arranging the scanning and posting of books and articles. Special thanks must go too to those good friends who filled lacunae from their own shelves: especially David Gilliland, Daniel Rudge, and Jonathan Seed, who dealt patiently and promptly with my importunities.

My debt to Sara and Josiah defies calculation, never mind expression. Suffice it to say that, without their support very little of what I do would be at all possible and I thank God for them both.

MARK SWEETNAM
Dublin, 2023.

Contents

	Introduction	9
	Outline	25
1	Chapter One	27
2	Chapter Two	63
3	Chapter Three	131
4	Chapter Four	167
	Bibliography	209

Except where otherwise indicated, all quotations from Scripture are taken from Thomas Newberry's edition of the Authorised (King James) Version.

Introduction

THE WRITINGS OF THE APOSTLE PAUL are remarkable for their variety. They include letters to churches and to individuals, letters written to recipients who were well known to the apostle, and to those that he had never met. Some were written with joy, some with tears, some with pastoral concern, and some with righteous anger. But none is so intimate or so urgent as Paul's second letter to a young man called Timothy.

The intimacy of that letter derives largely from the close relationship between the two men. In its opening verses, Paul addresses Timothy as his 'dearly beloved son' (1:2). That may mean, as is often suggested, that Paul was instrumental in seeing Timothy saved. But even if it does mean that, it means much more. It was customary in the first century for philosophers and teachers to refer to their disciples as 'sons'. When Paul uses the term of Timothy he is not just referring to an isolated event in the past, but to an ongoing relationship of instruction and imitation. Paul had poured much time and teaching into Timothy; Timothy had responded not only by grasping the truth that the apostle communicated but by developing a character that reflected the qualities that had marked Paul's life. In his faithfulness to and love for Paul he stood in contrast to 'all they which are in Asia' (1:15) who had turned away from the apostle as his message became more unpopular and association with him more dangerous.

There has been some debate about the precise nature of the context that made association with Paul so dangerous and distasteful a thing. Does the desertion of those who had previously followed Paul indicate just a – fairly understandable – reluctance to be identified with a convicted criminal, under sentence of death? Or, is it rather a result of an atmosphere of intense official hostility to, and persecution of, the fledgling religion of Christianity? Since thew time of Eusebius, the latter view has long been dominant. Paul's imprisonment has been seen against the background of the Neronian persecution that broke out in the aftermath of the burning of Rome. The execution of Paul and Peter, the two most prominent figures in the early church, was a first salvo in an official and general war against Christianity.[1] More recently, however, the historicity of a widespread Neronian persecution has been questioned, and the execution of Paul seen as a standalone event, a sentence motivated not by the fact that he was a Christian, but because he 'had been found guilty of creating unlawful and seditious disturbances in the province of Judaea'.[2] In reality, the implications of this important historiographical debate for our understanding of this epistle are limited. Whether as the outcome of an ordinary legal process or as a manifestation of the malign machinations of the Roman state, Paul was in prison, preparing for execution. It is this context, rather than a wider atmosphere of repression, that is such an important feature of this epistle.

---

[1] See, for a good representative account of this approach, W. H. C. Frend, 'Persecutions: Genesis and legacy', in M. M. Mitchell and F. M. Young (eds), *The Cambridge History of Christianity, 1: Origins to Constantine*, (Cambridge: Cambridge University Press, 2006), 503–523.

[2] Brent D. Shaw, 'The Myth of the Neronian Persecution', *The Journal of Roman Studies*, 105 (2015), 73–100, 78.

Paul's circumstances, with their loneliness and jeopardy add to the intimacy of the letter. They also give it its unique urgency. Paul is aware that the time of his departure is 'at hand' (4:6). Death is drawing near – soon he will be 'offered', his life poured out as a final act of worship to God. Conscious of this he writes to Timothy: this letter is Paul's final will and testament.

What could the apostle, imprisoned and alone, have to bequeath beyond a few books and parchments, and a worn-out coat, the *disjecta membra* of a life sacrificed to the spread of the gospel? Naturally speaking, he had no legacy worth the name to impart to Timothy. But Paul had long since abandoned the values of earth for those of heaven, and he was in no doubt about the worth of the treasure that he was leaving to Timothy. In this letter he describes it as 'what has been entrusted to me' (1:12, NET), and as 'that good thing' (v. 14). That precious deposit, that 'good thing' was 'the form of sound words' that he had already delivered to Timothy as a sacred trust, and which Timothy must now defend and deliver to a coming generation.

That was no small task and no light responsibility. It is difficult to imagine how Timothy must have felt after he had read this letter through for the first time. Each new re-reading (and there must surely have been many) would have presented him afresh with a task of appalling proportions and immense importance. Timothy must have felt crushed by the responsibility. He was, we must remember, a relatively young man, but no amount of birthdays – or of experience – would have been sufficient to make the burden any less than overwhelming.

Nor would that burden be made lighter by the circumstances that surrounded Timothy. Paul allows him to harbour no illusions about the challenge that they would pose. Timothy will face opposition from the world, but he will also face disappointment and even opposition from those who claimed to be believers. 'All they which are in Asia', including 'Phygellus and Hermogenes' (1:15) had turned away from Paul, and were no more likely to prove loyal to Timothy. Demas, too, had proved untrue, for he 'loved this present world' (4:10). Others, like Hymenaeus and Philetus, were propagating false teachings that were as noisome, as invasive, and as deathly as gangrene (2:16–18). Others, unnamed, but described as 'men of corrupt minds, reprobate concerning the faith' (3:8) would be covertly at work in the homes of the believers, picking off the weak and the vulnerable. And all of this betrayal and departure were only the beginning, for Timothy lived, as we still do, in 'last days', marked by 'perilous times', times of unrestrained ferocity when all that God approves of is attacked, and men love stuff and self, and not what is good (3:1–5).

Against this background, Paul makes it relentlessly clear that Timothy's will be a lonely task. Timothy is directly and personally addressed in this epistle. On 22 occasions (in the Greek text) Paul will use the second person singular pronoun, 'you'. Timothy is right in the apostolic firing line – there is no deflecting the personal, individual impact of this epistle. On three occasions Paul focuses more tightly still, using the expression *su de*, 'you however' (3:10, 14; 4:5, NET). On these occasions, Timothy stands isolated in the spotlight of Divine attention. Going with the flow is not an option, for the flow is away from God, away from Paul, and away from the truth. Timothy must stand as an individual, stand on his own, stand without the support of friends or the comfort of the crowd.

Wise pastor that he is, Paul is fully conscious of the burden that he is placing upon Timothy, and part of his purpose in this letter is to remind his son in the faith of the resources that are at his disposal as he seeks to discharge his responsibility. He reminds Timothy that he has been equipped (1:6), empowered (1:7, 14), and is enabled (2:1) by God. He has, moreover, the example of the apostle (3:10–12) to motivate and direct him. And in his heart, and in his mind, he has the God-breathed Scriptures which are able to furnish him fully to every good work. The responsibility is great, but the resources are greater still. Paul is not imparting to Timothy an impossible task – just one that is humanly impossible. Timothy succeeded because the power and the provision were not drawn from the wells of his own endurance and ingenuity but from the vast reservoir of Divine supply.

Timothy is to be more than just a doctrinal conveyor belt, receiving truth from the apostle, and dispensing it to others. Such a mechanical transmission of truth would be unprofitable, even if it were possible. It takes a godly man to be 'the man of God'. And so Paul writes to remind Timothy about the importance of his moral character. The preservation of that will require the man whose task in relation to truth is to stand fast and fight (2:3–4) to 'flee' (2:22), to 'shun' (2:16), and to 'avoid' (2:23). To do what Paul wants him to do – to do, in fact, what God wants him to do, Timothy will need to be pure morally and doctrinally – and to do that he will need to be different from all those around him.

AUTHOR

There would seem, on the face of it, little room for doubt that the Apostle Paul was the author, under the inspiration of the Holy Spirit, of this epistle. Not only is the very first word of the epistle 'Paul', but the verses that follow are full of autobiographical material and deeply personal reflection by the apostle on his life, ministry, and impending martyrdom. In the light of this, it is impossible to question, still less deny, that the epistle presents itself as an authentic letter from the Apostle Paul.

That might seem to be all that needs to be said on the issue, but anyone who has read very many commentaries on the epistle will know that a good deal more has been said. For, although the Pastoral Epistles (1 and 2 Timothy and Titus) have been accepted as genuine Pauline epistles throughout the history of Christianity, there have, since the end of the of the eighteenth century, been those who have denied that Paul is their author. Many scholars – including some of a generally conservative persuasion – now believe that Paul did not write the Pastoral Epistles. This belief is largely – though not exclusively – based on the language of these epistles. While critics have pointed to the difficulty of reconciling the account of Paul's travels in the Pastorals with what we know from the book of Acts and have alleged that the theology of these epistles differs from that of Paul's other epistles, their appeal is primarily to the unusual language of the Pastoral Epistles, when compared to Paul's other epistles.

Over recent decades, the tide of scholarly opinion has swung back in the direction of Pauline authorship.[3] More recently, rigorous statistical and linguistic analysis by Jermo van Nes has decisively demonstrated that linguistic variation does not provide a basis for questioning the Pauline authorship of the Pastoral Epistles.[4]

---

[3] A useful overview of this debate can be found in Philip H. Towner, *The Letters to Timothy and Titus*, The New International Commentary on the New Testament, (Grand Rapid, MI: Eerdmans, 2006), 9–26.

[4] Jermo van Nes, *Pauline Language and the Pastoral Epistles: A Study of Linguistic Variation in the Corpus Paulinum*, (Leiden: Brill, 2017).

In addition to claims of linguistic differences, some commentators have argued that there are significant theological differences between the Pastorals and the epistles definitely attributed to Paul. These arguments are subjective, and seem, at times, not to allow for Paul's teaching to have developed at all over the course of his ministry. So, for example, it has been argued that Paul's view of revelation in his early epistles as something dynamic and ongoing has been replaced by the view that revelation is static and fixed. And that is true – not because the author is different, but because the same author is writing at a different time, when the canon of Scripture is close to completion, and when all the major doctrines of the New Testament have been revealed. Others argue that the role of women in the Pastoral Epistles differs significantly from Paul's earlier epistles. This, however, is to ignore (or to avoid) 1 Corinthians 14:34,35, where Paul, in one of his earliest epistles gives very similar teaching. It has been suggested that the Pastoral Epistles address a version of Gnosticism too fully-fledged to have existed during Paul's lifetime. It must, however, be acknowledged that Paul goes out of his way to provide as little detail as possible about the error that Timothy and Titus will face, and what he does say could apply as well to the Judaizing error that we know to have been rife in the early church. And the argument that the presentation of church government in the Pastoral Epistles reflects something more ordered and formal than we see in the Acts or the epistles is difficult to sustain in the light of the fact that Paul, in Acts 20:17 was able to call 'the elders of the church' at Ephesus, or that he addressed the Philippian epistle 'to all the saints in Christ Jesus which are at Philippi, with the bishops and deacons' (1:1). These are all inescapably subjective arguments, and in the absence of strong linguistic evidence hardly seem sufficient to overcome the burden of proof upon those who differ from the clear testimony of the epistles and the belief of centuries of believers.

Having accepted the epistle's testimony to Pauline authorship, we must then answer the question of where these letters fit within the chronology of Paul's life and labours. From the book of the Acts, we know that Paul was arrested in Jerusalem (Acts 21), and sent to Caesarea, where he appeared before Felix and Festus (Acts 23–25). Having appealed to Caesar (Acts 25:11), and following a hazardous journey, he eventually arrived in Rome, where he 'was suffered to dwell by himself with a soldier that kept him' (Acts 28:16). The close of Acts finds the apostle under house arrest: 'And Paul dwelt two whole years in his own hired house, and received all that came in unto him, preaching the kingdom of God, and teaching those things which concern the Lord Jesus Christ' (Acts 28:30,31). It was during this period of imprisonment that he wrote his 'prison epistles': Ephesians, Philippians, Colossians, and Philemon. By the time he writes 2 Timothy, Paul is in prison, has appeared before Nero (2 Tim. 4:16), and is expecting his imminent execution. History tells us that execution took place at some time before the end of Nero's reign in AD 68.

Some commentators have argued that Paul was imprisoned only once, and that the Pastoral Epistles must have been written before (1 Timothy and Titus) and during (2 Timothy) his imprisonment in Rome. To accommodate the necessary movements, they suggest that there are gaps in the narrative of Acts – one commentator sees a gap of a year between Acts 19:20 and 21, for example. There is nothing inherently impossible about this suggestion and the strongest objection to it – that it is entirely speculative – can be made with almost equal force about the alternative. The difference in tone and content between the prison epistles and the Pastoral Epistles might also be regarded as a problem for this view.

It is, perhaps, less problematic to conclude that Paul was released from his Acts 28 imprisonment, carried out further missionary travels for two to three years, before being re-imprisoned, and that it was during the period between his release and execution that the Pastoral Epistles were written. This view allows ample time for Paul's travels as outlined in 1 Timothy and Titus – to Ephesus and Macedonia (1 Tim. 1:3), to Troas (2 Tim. 4:13), to Corinth and Miletum (4:20), and to Nicopolis (Tit. 3:12). It accommodates a visit to Crete (see Titus 1:5, although the language used may not demand a visit). It also allows time for Paul to achieve his ambition of bringing the gospel to Spain (Rom. 15). While this solution is nearly as speculative as the first, it is supported by tradition. Paul's visit to Spain is probably mentioned in a letter from Clement, which speaks of his travels to 'the limits of the West'.[5] It is also mentioned in the Muratorian Canon and in the apocryphal *Acts of Peter*. The fourth-century historian Eusebius tells us that Paul was released, carried out further missionary work, and was rearrested, and that during 'this imprisonment he wrote his second epistle to Timothy'.[6] It is difficult to know how far we can rely on tradition, but, for what it is worth, it weighs on the side of a second imprisonment.[7]

In summary then, when we come to 2 Timothy we have no need to imagine a pseudonymous writer mixing snippets of Paul's words with his own writing to concoct

---

[5] 1 *Clement* 5:7.
[6] Eusebius, of Caesarea, *Eusebius' Ecclesiastical History*, (trans. C.F. Cruse) (Peabody, MA: Hendrickson, 1998), 2.22.
[7] For a detailed attempt to reconstruct the chronology of the Pastoral Epistles see William D. Mounce, *Pastoral Epistles*, Word Biblical Commentary, (Nashville: Thomas Nelson Publishers, 2000), lv–lxiv.

a deception. We can stand firm on the testimony of Scripture. These words, inspired by the Holy Spirit, come to us from the pen, and the heart of the Apostle Paul and we can harbour no doubt as to their importance, their authority, and their enduring value.

THE RECIPIENT

Relay races are won in the handover. No swiftness on the part of the individual runners can compensate for fluffing that crucial moment when the baton passes from runner to runner. This is why relay teams spend hours practising until the handover is as clean and as certain as it can possibly be. 2 Timothy is about that point in the race of Christian testimony. Paul has run his stage well. Timothy is waiting to take his place. There has been no rehearsal of this handover and yet Timothy's entire Christian life had been spent in practice for this moment. It was a moment that called for a hero – or rather, for a man of God.

Timothy was not an obvious hero. Nothing in Scripture would make us think that he was an imposing, granite-jawed figure, broad at the shoulder, narrow at the hip, liberally equipped with confidence and charisma. Nor was his upbringing especially promising, for Timothy was raised in a mixed home: he was 'the son of a certain woman, which was a Jewess, and believed; but his father was a Greek' (Acts 16:1). Possibly because of this circumstance, his mother had not had him circumcised (Acts 16:3), but she had been faithful in teaching him 'the holy Scriptures' from his infancy (2 Tim. 3:15). His does not seem to have been a robust physiology – Paul encouraged him to 'use a little wine for thy stomach's sake, and thine often infirmities' (1 Tim. 5:23). This physical weakness seems to have been matched by a somewhat diffident personality, for Paul found it necessary to instruct the Corinthians to 'see that he may be with you without fear' (1 Cor. 16:10), and exhorted Timothy to 'let no man despise thy youth' (1 Tim. 4:12).

We must be careful not to overstate Timothy's weakness. To be parachuted into noisy, quarrelsome Corinth as a representative of the not-entirely-popular Apostle Paul, or to face down error in Ephesus, might have daunted the most robust personality. Certainly, it seems to be going well beyond the scope of the Biblical evidence to suggest that 'the cement of Timothy's character seems never to have really set'.[8] Timothy was not a superman – he had his failings and weaknesses just as we all do. But there was nothing spineless about him.

Timothy was not an obvious hero, not the sort of man that we might have expected God to use – unless we had read our Bibles. Scripture is full of unlikely heroes – of men without exceptional natural abilities being taken up by God, equipped by Him for their task, and sustained by Him as they carry it out. From Moses to Gideon to David, the Bible reminds us again and again: 'the Lord seeth not as man seeth; for man looketh on the outward appearance, but the Lord looketh on the heart' (1 Sam. 16:7). And Scripture reminds us too that God equips those whom He chooses, making His servants more than they were, or ever dreamed they could be.

God equipped Timothy for the task that lay ahead with a gift (1 Tim. 4:14; 2 Tim. 1:6) and with grace (2 Tim. 2:1). Something else was needed. Between his first appearance on the page of Scripture, in Acts 16, and 2 Timothy, Timothy had undergone a rigorous training that equipped and qualified him for his new responsibility. Timothy had proven himself worthy of Paul's confidence, as well his affection, and while the responsibility that was now placed upon him might have

---

[8] Harrington C. Lees, quoted in D. Edmond Hiebert, *Personalities Around Paul*, Chicago: Moody Press, 1973), 113.

surprised Timothy it would hardly have surprised those who knew him, for he had already demonstrated his suitability for the task. That should still be the case – while we may well be surprised ourselves by the responsibilities that we are given, there is something amiss if others are.

First and most fundamental of Timothy's qualifications was his 'unfeigned faith' (2 Tim. 1:5), a faith without hypocrisy. Such faith marked Timothy out amidst all of the hypocrisy of the false teachers, who had 'a form of godliness, but [denied] the power thereof' (2 Tim. 3:5). In that context, the value of Timothy's sincere faith shone all the clearer.

Timothy was qualified by his relationships. He was blessed with a godly mother and grandmother, and clearly their influence on Timothy was important. But more important than the relationships that Timothy was born into were those he chose. This is still true – the friendships that we make will both have an impact on, and serve as an index of, our spiritual development. Paul expected Timothy to be associated with 'faithful men' (2 Tim. 2:2), and they still make the best company for a believer.

There was, however, one relationship that dominated Timothy's life. That was his relationship with Paul. Like Moses and Joshua, Paul and Timothy stand testament to the value of relationships that cross the generations. 'Mentoring' has become part of business jargon in a way that makes the careful writer shy away from its use, but there is hardly a more apposite word to describe the relationship between the apostle and his 'son in the faith'. Like any successful mentorship, it was a reciprocal relationship. Paul invested time, energy, and patience in Timothy, and the letter before us shows that he did so with a pastoral care for the younger man's wellbeing.

And Timothy responded to Paul's efforts as wholeheartedly as any teacher could desire.

It may be that this mentoring of a younger generation by an older and more experienced one is a significant area of weakness for us. If that is so, the blame lies with both generations. The older generation needs to learn from Paul, and the younger from Timothy. It is a sad and a dangerous thing to see old pitted against young, mutually intolerant and mutually dismissive. Such an attitude will be of no help to the transmission of truth and the maintenance of testimony, and we should be very cautious about doing anything to create or to foster a divide between the generations.

Timothy learned much from the apostle Paul. But it is clear that he was also a careful student of the Word of God. He had learned the Old Testament Scriptures at his mother's knee, and Paul was confident in his grasp of New Testament revelation. So, he could speak to Timothy of 'the things that thou hast heard of me among many witnesses' (2 Tim. 2:2). To put it (slightly anachronistically) in the language of today, Timothy knew his Bible. That is still an essential requirement for those that God will use. Any young believer who desires to serve God and to help his people will need to emulate Timothy in getting a firm grasp on the Scriptures, and forming individual and personal convictions about what it is that they teach.

Timothy was also marked by exertion. Paul spoke of him as his 'workfellow' (Rom. 16:21, 1 Thess. 3:2) and as the servant of Jesus Christ (Phil. 1:1), who 'worketh the work of the Lord' (1 Cor. 16:10). Timothy was not afraid to work, and he exerted himself in the Lord's service. While we do need to be careful not to make the mistake of thinking that there is something inherently meritorious in mere busyness, his example reminds us that lazy men and women are of little use to God – those who would serve Him must be prepared to serve.

Finally, Timothy was qualified by his attitude to the Lord's people. One of the loveliest of the commendations that he received from Paul is recorded in Philippians 2:20: 'I have no one like-minded who will care with genuine feeling how ye get on' (JND). Timothy was a man who cared deeply for the welfare of God's people, who was genuinely interested in and concerned for their spiritual wellbeing and progress. He was firm, but he was never hard, and when he had to 'reprove, rebuke, exhort' (2 Tim. 4:2), his listeners would always have been conscious that the words of censure came from a loving heart. It should be so for us too.

Timothy was a remarkable man. But his spiritual character and his spiritual capacity were formed in just the same way that ours are – one day at a time. It is likely that he never expected to receive a letter like 2 Timothy, but when it came he was ready, We do not know what service and responsibility lies before us. But we can make sure that, when God calls us, we are ready for the Master's use.

Approach

2 Timothy opens with an address to 'Timothy, my dearly beloved son', but it closes with a benediction addressed with a plural pronoun: 'Grace be with you' (4:22). This commentary takes the epistle seriously as a personal letter addressed by Paul to Timothy, his intimate associate, and carefully crafted by the apostle to encourage, exhort, and equip the man whose responsibility it will be to carry on Paul's work after his death. But it also seeks to pay due attention to the hint of the epistle's closing words: this is not just a personal epistle and Paul speaks, through Timothy, to a far wider audience.

With this in view, the goal of this commentary is both to expound the epistle and to apply it. Though it is draws on the scholarship that has so helpfully illuminated our understanding of the epistle, and while it is intended to make a contribution to that scholarship, it does not aim at being just a scholarly examination of an interesting historical text. Rather, it takes seriously 2 Timothy's function as a work of paraenesis, as a text crafted to produce practical, as well as intellectual, results in its readers.

Like so many of the books in our Bible, 2 Timothy is they intensely particular and occasional. Whether we think of the Old Testament prophets or the letter writers of the New Testament, we are dealing with documents written by and to people in geographical and chronological contexts that are miles and years from us. 2 Timothy, addressed to one man in a very special set of circumstances and expressing a very special relationship, is more particular still. And yet, like the prophecies of Isaiah, or the histories of Ezra, it transcends the circumstances and contexts of its writing and speaks with immediacy, relevance, and power to the present day.

That is not, perhaps, entirely surprising, for we live in a world that, while superficially very different from Timothy's, is really just the same. We are still living in last days. Truth is still under attack. Christians still turn away from obedience to the Word of God because the world and the price of discipleship are both too dear. But the God Who Paul served 'from [his] forefathers' (1:3), is still at work. And He still needs individuals – men and women both – who are prepared to stand out from the crowd, shoulder the burden of truth, hold it fast in their own generation, and pass it unaltered to the succeeding generation. The task is still beyond human ability. But

Divine equipment, empowering, and enabling are still available. And the Scriptures still are able to completely complete us to every good work. There is, perhaps, no better summary of this epistle than the words of Psalm 100:5, as rendered in verse by William Kethe:

The Lord our God is good;
His mercy is for ever sure;
His truth at all times firmly stood,
And shall from age to age endure.

OUTLINE

CHAPTER 1

1:1–2	SALUTATION	
1:3–7	THE APPRECIATION AND APPOINTMENT OF THE MAN OF GOD	
	vv. 2–5	A venerable inheritance
	vv. 6–7	A vital impartation
1:8–18	THE ATTITUDE OF THE MAN OF GOD	
	vv. 8–14	Exhorted
	vv. 15–18	Exemplified

CHAPTER 2

2:1–13	THE ANTICIPATION OF THE MAN OF GOD	
	vv. 1–7	Service and the future
	vv. 8–10	Saints and the future
	vv. 11–13	Suffering and the future
2:14–26	THE ACTIVITIES OF THE MAN OF GOD	
	vv. 14–15	Studying
	vv. 16–18	Shunning
	vv. 19–21	Sanctification
	vv. 22–26	Service

CHAPTER 3

3:1–17	THE AWARENESS OF THE MAN OF GOD	
	vv. 1–9	The fierceness of the times
	vv. 10–13	The faithfulness of the apostle
	vv. 14–17	The fulness of the Scriptures

CHAPTER 4

4:1–8   THE ALERTNESS OF THE MAN OF GOD
- v. 1 — The solemnity of the charge
- v. 2 — The scope of the charge
- vv. 3–4 — The season of the charge
- vv. 5–8 — The span of the charge

4:9–21   THE ASSOCIATES OF THE MAN OF GOD
- vv. 9–10a — Disappointing associates
- vv. 10b–13 — Diligent associates
- vv. 14–15 — Damaging associates
- vv. 16–18 — Divine assistance
- vv. 19–21 — Dear associates

4:22   CLOSING GREETING AND PRAYER

Chapter One

1:1–2 Salutation

ANYONE WHO STUDIED A LANGUAGE in school is likely to have spent some time learning how to write a letter. There is a reason for this, which has more to do with the formulaic nature of letters than any real likelihood of needing to carry on a correspondence with a foreign pen pal. What is true of modern letters was also true of those written in the first century – only the form has changed. A Greek letter opened with the name of the author, followed by that of the recipient, and a salutation: Paul to Timothy, greeting. This skeleton clearly lies behind the opening to this epistle but Paul, very typically, has considerably fleshed out each of the sections, so that the opening is not merely formulaic but exceedingly important for our understanding of the epistle that follows it.

Verse 1 Paul begins the epistle with a statement of his apostleship. That he does so here, and in the other Pastoral Epistles has puzzled some readers. We can readily understand why Paul stresses his authority in contexts where it is being challenged, but why does he mention it here, in a personal letter, to his loyal son? There are at least two answers to this question. Firstly, Timothy was being given a solemn charge, and is being reminded that it comes not just from his beloved father in the faith, but from the apostle, with apostolic authority. But the remainder was not just for Timothy.

As the plural pronoun of the letter's closing sentence ('Grace be with you' 4:22) demonstrates, this epistle was not for Timothy's eyes only, and those who read it would have been reminded not only of Paul's authority, but of Timothy's. And, of course, Paul was writing under the inspiration of the Holy Spirit, and the reminder of the authority of this letter underscores its importance for us.

Paul adds two details about his apostleship – it is 'by the will of God, according to the promise of life which is in Christ Jesus'. Both of these expressions have a particular poignancy when we keep in mind the circumstances in which Paul wrote the epistle. From a human standpoint, these were dire. Paul was friendless and forsaken, a condemned prisoner confined in a Roman prison and awaiting execution. This was not how anyone expected the story to end – the contrast between the glory of the Damascus road and the dank darkness of the Mamertine prison could hardly be more striking. In these circumstances, Timothy might well have asked what had gone wrong, and Paul is reassuring him that, in truth, nothing had had. He was an apostle 'by the will of God' and everything that he was experiencing lay within the embrace of the Divine will. Not only so, but it was in conformity with 'the promise of life which is in Christ Jesus'. It didn't look like it – the apostle was about to die. But as death grew closer, the promise of life shone brighter, and it is that promise – and the hope that it brings – that Paul identifies as the correct metric by which to evaluate his apostleship.

'According to the promise of life which is in Christ Jesus' is a difficult expression fully to understand. Some translations, and quite a few commentators, will translate 'according' (*kata*) as 'for the sake of', 'with a view to', and, on the basis of this reading, suggest that Paul 'had been commissioned as an apostle first to formulate and then to communicate the gospel'.[1] There is some truth in this – though 'formulate' is not a very happy choice of word here – but it is more likely that it is 'not the object and the intention of the apostleship [that] are expressed thereby, but its character'.[2] Paul is reminding Timothy that his calling is in keeping with the promise of life. And we should not allow debate about the beginning of the clause to cause us to miss the glorious truth of its conclusion – both the promise and the eternal life are found 'in Christ Jesus' (*cf.* v. 11). In this first verse of the epistle, Paul has outlined his Divine mandate for the charge that follows.

Verse 2 Paul then describes the recipient of the letter: 'Timothy, my dearly beloved son'. Clearly, the language used communicates great affection and intimacy – this would seem to be a warmer greeting than 1 Timothy's 'my own son in the faith' (1 Tim. 1:2). It has often been suggested that Paul's use of 'son' means that Timothy became a Christian as a result of the apostle's preaching. This may well be so, but the significance of the description goes well beyond that, for it describes an ongoing relationship. With that relationship comes responsibility. As Paul's son, Timothy would be expected to bear a resemblance to him – his character should be compatible with that of his spiritual father. And the fact that the solemn charges to Timothy in this epistle come from a father to a son lends them tremendous weight – Paul is reminding Timothy of an obligation that cannot be evaded.

---

[1] John Stott, *The Bible Speaks Today: The Message of 2 Timothy*, (Nottingham: Inter-Varsity Press, 1999), 24.
[2] William Kelly, *An Exposition of the Two Epistles to Timothy* 3rd ed., (London: C.A. Hammond, 1948), 181. Our understanding of this verse is likely to be informed by our view of Titus 1:1 and *vice versa*.

Paul's greeting – 'Grace, mercy, and peace, from God our Father and Christ Jesus our Lord' (1:2; *c.f.* 1 Tim. 1:2, *JND*) – is unique to the epistles to Timothy. It is only in these two epistles that the title 'Christ Jesus our Lord' is used. 'Caesar is Lord' was the cry of the Roman cult of emperor worship. Paul's imprisonment and execution were part of Nero's programme of persecution, and one of the key justifications of that persecution was the Christian's refusal to join in that idolatrous and blasphemous cry. Here, at the beginning of the letter, Paul reminds Timothy who really is Lord.[3] And He is 'our Lord', just as God is 'our Father'. In the verses that follow Paul will be very frank about the cost of faithfulness to God, and identification with Christ. But that cost – real though it is – pales by comparison with the glorious truth that God is 'our Father', and the exalted 'Christ Jesus' is 'our Lord'. That privilege brings inevitable and concomitant responsibility – the claims of Divine persons upon our obedience and our faithfulness cannot be disregarded or denied.

Grace and peace are standard elements of Paul's salutations, but only in the epistles to Timothy (and Titus, if we follow the *Textus Receptus*) does the opening prayer mention mercy. This may well speak to the context in which these men laboured – a possibility that is borne out by Paul's prayer for mercy for Onesiphorus and his household later in this chapter (1:16, 18). Mercy 'is a form of love determined by the state or condition of its objects'.[4] In the circumstances faced by Timothy and Titus, God's mercy would be a precious resource, and one that would be required daily. Here, as always, grace

---

[3] We can see a similar emphasis in the use of 'Saviour', another title claimed by Caesar, in the Pastoral Epistles.

[4] Miley, quoted in Merrill F. Unger, *The New Unger's Bible Dictionary*, ed. R.K. Harrison, (Chicago: Moody Press, 1988), *s.v.*

comes first, 'the general term for that energy and outflow of divine goodness which rises above man's evil and ruin, and loves notwithstanding all'.[5] It is the basis for the other blessings that are mentioned. God's grace and God's mercy issue in a peace that is independent of circumstances.

It is easy to pass over the opening verses of New Testament epistles as though they were merely routine. However, nothing in Scripture is routine or redundant, and that is certainly true of these two verses. Within their brief compress, Paul outlines his right to instruct Timothy, the relationship that underlies that instruction, and the resources that will enable Timothy to put these instructions into operation. In addition, he establishes the atmosphere of love and affection that is so distinctive of this lovely letter. And he addresses the key themes of the epistle: the power of God, and the confidence that it brings, the importance and reliability of the gospel, and the hope that it brings, and the certainty of victory in spite of every indication to the contrary. As we continue to explore this epistle we will watch the seeds sown in these verses grow and blossom into a glorious display of precious truth.

1:3–7: THE APPRECIATION AND APPOINTMENT OF THE MAN OF GOD

vv. 3–5   **A Venerable Inheritance**

Verse 3 The prayer life of the apostle Paul is a helpful – if very humbling – topic of study. Although we should remember that Paul's epistles show us only fragmented slices of the apostle's prayer, and although we must be alert to the dangers of extrapolating too wildly from

---

[5] Kelly, *Exposition*, 184.

what is recorded, we have enough to make us feel that our own prayer is dilatory and disorganised.

Paul's prayer was striking for its consistency. That is clear in the verses that we are presently considering. The expression 'without ceasing I have remembrance of thee in my prayers night and day' does not mean that Paul was constantly praying – that would be a physical impossibility. Rather, he is letting Timothy know that, whenever he prays, Timothy's name is mentioned and Timothy's need remembered. The expression 'night and day' suggests that Paul had a disciplined and orderly prayer life, and it is only such a prayer life that could explain a life of service like his.

Paul's prayer is striking for its content, as well as for its consistency. In a general way, we could learn a great deal from the priorities that his prayer reveals – his concern for the spiritual growth of believers, for the unity of assemblies, and for the progress of the gospel should surely dominate our prayers too. But, more specifically, an examination of the opening prayers of Paul's epistles reveals how carefully and intelligently he prayed. There is nothing *pro forma* about the prayers recorded: rather, they engage intelligently with the content of each epistle and the needs of the audience addressed.[6]

This is certainly the case in 2 Timothy. Paul's prayer of thanksgiving anticipates much of the material that follows. The example of Paul's faithfulness, the significance of his relationship with Timothy, and Timothy's spiritual biography all feature in this prayer, and will remain important throughout the epistle.

In addition to this, Paul's references in these verses to his own spiritual heritage and to Timothy's background

---

[6] The classic study of this topic is Peter O'Brien, *Introductory Thanksgivings in the Letters of Paul*, (Eugene, OR: Wipf and Stock, 2009). Regrettably, O'Brien omits the Pastoral Epistles from his study.

serve both to provide a basis for the charge that he issues to Timothy and to underscore the importance of that charge. Timothy is being reminded that the legacy that is being entrusted to him is not something of recent origin. In a society that equated antiquity with importance, Timothy needs to appreciate that he is not handling a recent innovation. Rather, he finds himself part of a venerable heritage that goes back beyond him, beyond his grandparents, and beyond that again to the forefathers. Timothy has become part of Divine history. And so have we. The truth that we hold matters. It is not a novelty, some recent invention whose fate ultimately makes no difference. It is a venerable and valuable inheritance. Compared to Timothy, we inherit two additional millennia of Christian testimony, and the truth that we hold has come to our hands not just from the apostle, or from Timothy, but from generations of our brothers and sisters who have received the truth, preserved it, and passed it on. Shame on us if we should lightly value their investment and be the generation that handles the inheritance carelessly. The study of history has its hazards, but in its place it has much to offer us, for it prevents us from either under- or overestimating the importance of our role in the programme of God.

It is for this reason that Paul speaks about serving – the word has connotations of worship – God 'from my forefathers with pure conscience'. Some have taken this as a reference to Paul's service before his conversion, a view which requires some explanation of the phrase 'with pure conscience', when we consider 1 Timothy 1:12–16. However, as the present tense 'serve' indicates, Paul is thinking here of his ongoing service of God, whom he serves 'as my forefathers did' (NIV). For all the dispensational change that has taken place, there remains an essential continuity between Paul's service and that of his forebears – he is serving the same God, in the same way. We should not miss the fact that Paul served 'with pure conscience' (v. 3). That is vitally important in light of all that this epistle has to say about shame. Although men might be ashamed to be identified with Paul, in his imprisonment and disgrace (1:15), and although even loyal and loving Timothy had to be exhorted not to be ashamed (1:8), Paul knew that he had nothing to be ashamed about.

Because Timothy is Paul's son, he enters into this inheritance but he also had a heritage of his own: 'the unfeigned faith that is in thee, which dwelt first in thy grandmother Lois, and thy mother Eunice; and I am persuaded that in thee also'. In addition, it is worth noting that Timothy is a third-generation believer. As a third-generation believer, I remember feeling rather resentful of brethren who reminded us that the third generation has a rather poor Biblical reputation. But, however unpalatable, there was truth in what they said. Often, the convictions formed and the ground gained by the first generation are undervalued by the second generation, and let slip by the third. However, this is not inevitable: Timothy's example should encourage and challenge third generation believers – and believers of every other generation too.

Timothy came from a mixed home: there is no suggestion in Scripture that his father was a Christian. But Timothy's character had been formed by the faithful efforts of two godly women. The mention of their names here, along with the reference to Timothy's education in 3:15, gives us a little glimpse of their importance in his life. Their work was carried out in the domestic sphere, but its value should not be underestimated. The Pastoral Epistles, as a whole, stress the importance of the home in the maintenance of testimony, and here, in 2 Timothy, we see that importance clearly exemplified. They stress, too, the contribution that can be made by sisters, and that, too, is clearly illustrated by Lois and Eunice. We should never be so foolish as to discount or devalue the service of sisters, just because it is private and domestic in its setting.

Paul's prayer, then, is highly strategic in the context of this epistle. But it is no merely formal, if effective, rhetorical flourish. Rather, it is deeply personal and affective, revealing not just Paul's emotions, but Timothy's too. The prayer is couched as thanksgiving – Paul is grateful for the friendship, fellowship, and faithfulness of a man like Timothy. It is not difficult to understand this – both Timothy's personal qualities and his faithfulness against the background of a general desertion of the apostle were a cause for thanksgiving. Moreover, such thanksgiving is characteristic of the apostle; a man who always appreciated other believers and the contribution that they could make.

Paul's appreciation of Timothy was clearly reciprocated. We do not know when it was that Timothy wept, but it seems likely that Paul is here remembering some parting, or partings, when Timothy's tears registered his regard for the apostle and his regret at being parted from him. Certainly, Paul anticipates their reunion will bring joy – indeed he anticipates being 'filled with joy' by Timothy's presence (v. 4).

These verses are all about the past and, like many an aged saint, Paul's mind is occupied with his memories – something that is emphasised by the three references to remembering in verses 3–5 (translated 'mindful' in verse 4). But these are no idle reminiscences. Paul is looking to the past with the future in mind and, as we make our way through the chapter, his focus turns to the future. His balance is worthy of emulation. We can too readily ignore the past, just as we can too often become obsessed by it. Dan Crawford, the pioneer missionary to Africa, took as his motto the phrase 'hats off to the past; coats off to the future'.[7] Paul would surely have agreed.

These few verses abound with lessons for us. They remind us of the value of consistent, thankful prayer for our fellow believers. They offer us an example of Christian love and fellowship, undiminished by generational difference. They raise a monument to two godly sisters and underscore for all of us the value of the domestic and private service of sisters, which is too often overlooked by men – and by women too – but which is recognised and recorded by God. And they reinforce for us the importance of understanding where we stand in history and the value of the inheritance that we have received – and that we must keep.

vv. 6, 7   A Vital Impartation

As we have seen, Paul's prayer for Timothy (1:3–5) stresses the closeness of the relationship between the two men. These are precious topics to consider but, as qualifications for the service of God, neither relationships nor feelings are sufficient. Even Timothy's faith, sincere as it was, was not enough by itself. Something more is required and, in this section, Paul outlines two resources that Timothy has received, and that qualify him for his task: 'the gift of God' (v. 6) and the Spirit 'of power, and of love, and of a sound mind' (v. 7). There has been some debate about both of these verses, and we will need to consider them in some detail.

Verse 6 The word 'gift' in this verse is the Greek word *charisma*. It is linked by etymology to the word 'grace'

---

[7] James J. Ellis, *Dan Crawford of Luanza*, (Kilmarnock: John Ritchie, n.d.), 94.

(*charis*) and describes a 'gracious endowment'[8] or 'a favour which one receives without any merit of his own'.[9] It is the word that is used in Romans 12, 1 Corinthians 12, and (I would argue) 1 Peter 4:10 of spiritual gifts, of Divine enablement for the service of God, beyond any talents and abilities that we have by birth, education, or training. Although that meaning seems to fit the context and the language of this verse very well, not all interpreters are convinced that it is this sort of gift that is in view here.

The mention of laying on of hands leads some commentators (generally those with a particular set of ecclesiastical presuppositions) to conclude that ordination is in view.[10] A similar view dismisses any notion of ecclesiastical ordination but argues that the gift in view here should be understood as a calling or ministry.[11] There are considerable difficulties with both of these views, in relation to both the context and the contents of the verse. As we have already seen, the context of these verses is the encouragement of Timothy by reminding him of the resources that God has provided to enable him for the responsibility that lay before him. Before he outlines the task Paul is reassuring Timothy that he has been provided with the ability and the energy to discharge it. But the more serious difficulty comes from the words of the verse. Paul urges Timothy to 'stir up' his gift, to fan it into flame. It is difficult to see

---

[8] Gordon D. Fee, *1 & 2 Timothy, Titus,* Understanding the Bible Commentary Series, (Grand Rapids, MI: Baker Books, 1988), 108.
[9] Joseph Henry Thayer, *Thayer's Greek Lexicon of the New Testament,* (Grand Rapids: Baker Book House, 1977), *s.v.*
[10] See, for example, J.N.D. Kelly, *A Commentary on the Pastoral Epistles,* (London: A. & C. Black, 1963), 159–160.
[11] See Kenneth Berding, *What are Spiritual Gifts? Rethinking the Conventional View,* (Grand Rapids, MI: Kregel, 2006), 59–60. Even by the standards of this book, the treatment of 1 Timothy 4:14 and 2 Timothy 1:6 is strikingly tendentious.

how this language could be used of an ecclesiastical office or of a ministry. Secondly, Paul says that the gift is 'in you', using the same preposition that he used in verse 5 of the 'faith that is in thee'. Again it is difficult to understand how an office or a ministry can be said to be 'in' someone.[12]

Other commentators argue that verses 6 and 7 are both talking about the same thing – the imparting of the Holy Spirit.[13] This view has no difficulty with 'in you', which it sees simply as a reference to the indwelling of the Holy Spirit. Like the spiritual gift view, it seems to encounter some difficulty with the laying on of hands, but proponents generally agree with the view outlined below – that the laying on of hands involves recognition, rather than impartation. But the stirring up, or the fanning into flame, remains a difficulty, for it is not clear how this could be said of the Holy Spirit – Marshall's suggestion that 1 Thessalonians 5:19's 'quench not the Spirit' offers a parallel expression is unconvincing.[14]

The third view is that this verse, along with 1 Timothy 4:14, is referring to a spiritual gift in the same sense as Romans 12, 1 Corinthians 12, and 1 Peter 4:10.[15] This fits the context well and encounters no difficulties with either 'stirring up' the gift, or the gift being 'in you'. Timothy is to use his spiritual gift to the fullest extent possible, for it is a crucial element of his qualification to

---

[12] It is no solution to dismiss *en* as 'a little preposition' (Berding, *What are Spiritual Gifts?*, 292). The premise that only big words matter is hardly a safe or sensible foundation for exegesis.

[13] See, for example, Towner, *Timothy*, 458, and I. Howard Marshall, *The Pastoral Epistles*, International Critical Commentary, (Edinburgh: T&T Clark, 1999), 697, though he also suggests that 'The force is that the charisma for ministry, one of the specific charismata associated with the Spirit was conveyed to Timothy.'

[14] Marshall, *Pastoral Epistles*, 697.

[15] For examples of this view see Fee, *1 & 2 Timothy*, 226, and William D. Mounce, *Pastoral Epistles*, 476, 477.

be God's man – and Paul's. It is a general principle of Scriptural interpretation that the simplest interpretation is usually correct. When a view of a passage has to pile up special pleadings we justly regard it with some suspicion. Undoubtedly the simplest view of this passage is that it is speaking of Divinely endowed spiritual enablement. This gives full weight to the context and content of the verse and interprets *charismata* in a way that is consistent with wider Pauline usage.

That having been said, there remain two issues in the verse that we need briefly to consider. Firstly, we need to ask why Paul urges Timothy to 'stir up' his gift? Is there a suggestion here that Timothy was neglecting his gift? It is certainly the case that gift can be neglected – left idle and undeveloped, rather than being fanned into flame for God. This is by no means uncommon – the tragedy of undeveloped gift affects many believers – and many assemblies too. But we do not need to imagine that this was true of Timothy or that there is an implicit rebuke in Paul's words. The call to kindle up the flame of Timothy's gift most likely reflects, not a dwindling flame, but a necessary response to meet circumstances that were more difficult and challenges that were more acute.

The other issue that needs to be addressed is what Paul means by 'by the putting on of my hands'. Is he describing the impartation of spiritual gift, perhaps with a unique apostolic authority that is no longer in operation? Some interpreters have thought so,[16] but it is more likely that recognition and identification, rather than impartation are in view. Our understanding of the preposition 'by' (Gr *dia*) is clearly crucial to our understanding of the verse. If *dia* is instrumental – which it certainly could be – then Paul seems to be describing the communication of the spiritual gift. More

---

[16] Including Kelly, *Exposition*, 186, 187.

probably, however, it is used in this verse as 'the *dia* of attendant circumstances', expressing 'the circumstances that accompany an action or a state'.[17] The laying on of Paul's hands – which likely happened at the same time as that of the elders (1 Tim. 4:14) – did not impart anything, but it demonstrated the apostle's recognition of Timothy's gift and his identification of him as a qualified co-worker and successor. There may be an echo here of Numbers 27:18, where Moses is instructed by God to lay his hands on Joshua, thus identifying him to the nation as his successor.

Paul's exhortation to Timothy should prompt each one of us to search our consciences. We all have a gift – 1 Peter 4:10 could hardly make that clearer. But whether that gift has been fanned into flame is another matter. Kindling up a gift is costly – there may be rubbish that obstructs the flame and that will need to be removed. The fuel of energy, effort, and time must be supplied – no small cost in a world where our every minute seems to be mortgaged. But far better to make the effort and pay the price now, before we give account to Christ for a stewardship that has squandered the gift that He gave.

Nor should we miss Paul's willingness to recognise, encourage, and endorse Timothy's gift. How we respond to the gift of others – especially if they are younger than we – is an acid test of our spiritual maturity. Paul passed with flying colours – would that we might too!

Timothy, then, has been equipped for his task by 'the gift of God' (v. 6). He has also received the 'spirit ... of power, and of love, and of a sound mind' (v. 7). The quotation here follows the capitalisation used in the KJV, which suggests that it is Timothy's own spirit that is in view here. However, whether that is the case or not is

---

[17] Murray J. Harris, *Prepositions and Theology in the Greek New Testament*, (Grand Rapids, MI: Zondervan, 2012), 77.

worth exploring in a little detail, for quite a number of commentators have seen here a reference to the Holy Spirit. Before examining this, it is worth pointing out that the practical difference between these two views is minimal. Whether we are thinking about the Holy Spirit or Timothy's own spirit, it is clearly God who is the source of the 'power, ... love, ... a sound mind'. Directly or indirectly we see the Holy Spirit at work in this verse.

The link between the Holy Spirit and these attributes is one that Paul makes elsewhere (*cf.* e.g. Rom. 5:5; 15:13, 19; 1 Cor. 2:4; Gal. 5:22, 23). This link is perhaps the strongest argument for seeing a reference to the Holy Spirit in this verse. Also worthy of note is the parallel with Romans 8:15 ('For ye have not received the spirit of bondage again to fear; but ye have received the Spirit of adoption') which is similar linguistically, structurally, and grammatically, and which is quite definitely speaking of the Holy Spirit. The fact that the words for 'bondage' (*douleias*) and 'fear', or cowardice (*deilias*) are so similar in sound makes an allusion to the earlier verse the more likely.

The use of *deilias* in the verse leads Philip Towner to suggest another parallel, this time with Joshua 1:9: 'Have not I commanded thee? Be strong and of a good courage; be not afraid [*deiliasēs*], neither be thou dismayed: for the LORD thy God is with thee whithersoever thou goest.' Although he admits that the echo is faint, he argues that 'the tone, narrative setting, and intention of the instructions create a plausible match', especially given other verbal connections between the two accounts.[18]

Paul has already stressed the reality of Timothy's conversion and the reality of his 'unfeigned faith'. Because he is truly born again, he has received the Holy Spirit. 'The Spirit God gave us does not make us timid,

---

[18] Towner, *Timothy*, 460–461.

but gives us power, love and self-discipline' (NLT), and so Timothy is empowered for the daunting task that lies before him. To carry out that task would call on all of these resources – the power to carry out difficult spiritual labour, the love that would keep him from becoming embittered or hard in the face of opposition, and the self-discipline (or rationality, prudence, clearness of thought, restraint) that would be so vital in a world of distortion and deception. Indeed, the latter term is part of a group of words that reoccur throughout the Pastoral Epistles, and especially in the epistle to Titus (see 1 Tim. 2:9, 15; 3:2; Tit. 1:8; 2:2,4,5, 6, 12). The quality was praised in secular Greek writing but in these epistles it is explicitly identified as an attribute displayed by Christians. Clear thinking and self-discipline were important for Timothy and Titus, and they are just as important for believers in the twenty-first century.

And, of course, they are accessible to us. We may not have precisely the same gift that Timothy had, but we have the same Spirit. Each of us can say that God has not given us a spirit of fear, but the Spirit of love, power, and a sound mind. Wherever he has placed us, whatever work we have to do, and whatever challenges we face, we have within us the Spirit of God, enabling and energising us so that we do not need to be afraid.

In these two verses we have seen Timothy's equipping – a God-given gift and the God-given Spirit. It is because Timothy is equipped like this that the apostle can go on to the command that is given in the remainder of the chapter.

1:8–18 THE ATTITUDE OF THE MAN OF GOD

vv. 8–12 Exhorted

In the Greek text of this epistle, verses 8–12 form a single sentence. Verse 8 gives a double command, which is expanded upon in the verses that follow. The command is linked to what has gone before – notice the 'therefore'. The choice that faces Timothy in these verses will require his reliance on the resources provided by the Holy Spirit to overcome shame and to accept suffering. That reliance is stressed in this verse – Timothy is to be 'partaker of the afflictions of the gospel according to the power of God'. That vital closing clause has two implications. Firstly, Timothy was not to make the mistake that his afflictions for the gospel demonstrated any lack of Divine power. Power and persecution seem incompatible to us, but not to God. Secondly, Paul is once again reminding Timothy that the power to willingly endure persecution will be drawn, not from the cisterns of his own personality, resilience, and endurance, but from the vast and inexhaustible reservoir of Divine power.

The double command has a negative component – 'be not ashamed' and a positive 'be thou partaker of the afflictions of the gospel'. These instructions stand in opposition to each other. Timothy could be ashamed of the gospel and of Paul and desert the apostle, just as 'all they which are in Asia' had done (1:15), sacrificing loyalty to God for an easy life. Or he could stand by the gospel, stand by Paul, and partake in suffering. There was no middle way: the choice was as stark as that. The same choice still faces us. We may, for the time being – and it may be only for the time being – enjoy freedom from the sort of persecution that Paul was experiencing and that Timothy faced. But faithfulness to God and to His Word always comes at a price.

Paul makes no bones about the reality of that price – he is calling Timothy to be a 'partaker of the afflictions of the gospel'. 'Partaker of the afflictions' translates a single Greek word which Paul seems to have coined.

Timothy is to be a *synkakopatheō*, a 'together-sufferer' for the gospel.

Some commentators, as they expound 'be not ashamed', say a good deal about the 'shame culture' of the Hellenic world of the first century. Sometimes, they give the impression that this needs to be explained because our culture is somehow different. It isn't. We all care deeply about what people think of us. Christians are not immune from our society's obsession with projecting the right image, looking the right way, saying the right things. Whether or not we would use the word (and we shouldn't), we all want to be cool. And it is this desire to fit in, to belong, to be 'normal', that gives shame its power.

This is why shame is such a problem for Christians, because we are called to be different. The principles, the priorities, and the passions of our life are – and should be – radically different from those of our unsaved family, classmates, fellow students, and colleagues. We stand out, and because we stand out the world will do everything in its power to make us ashamed, so that we will conform, so that we will no longer be irritatingly, rebukingly different.

Every believer will have experienced this to some degree. But imagine now that, in addition to all the mockery and scorn that you faced in the classroom, you were friends with an older believer who was imprisoned for the sake of the gospel. Imagine that he had been convicted, not of some minor offence, but of a crime that your friends thought of as akin to murder. Imagine what it would be like to visit him – to enter the prison, to feel the disdain radiating from the guards and ringing out, with less restraint, from the lips of every criminal in every cell that you passed. Imagine fearing that the door that had opened to let you enter would not open to let you out. Would you still go? Would you choose not to be ashamed, but to be a fellow partaker 'of the afflictions of the gospel'? That was the choice that Paul expected Timothy to make and, in the following verses he reminds Timothy – and us – just why the right choice, though difficult, was obvious.

Verse 9 expands upon the double charge given by Paul to Timothy in verse 8. Drawing on Divine power, Timothy was not to be ashamed of the gospel or of Paul, but, by contrast, to be a 'co-sufferer' for the gospel. Such a prospect was far from attractive, but, in this verse, Paul begins to explain why it is the only course open to the Christian. His charge to suffer unashamed is motivated and mandated by the tremendous reality of what God has done for us: 'Who hath saved us, and called us with an holy calling, not according to our works, but according to his own purpose and grace'.

Throughout the Roman Empire, Caesar was hailed as a Saviour. Any fealty that he might demand, any taxation that he might levy, any restriction that he might impose was justified by his status as the Saviour, who had brought the benefits and blessings of Rome to the peoples of the Empire. There was a logic to the loyalty of his subjects. There is a logic to our loyalty too, for God has saved us. Our salvation is not political, temporary, and provisional. It is personal, eternal, and final. In the face of such blessing, shame has no place, infidelity would be irrational.

He saved us. Every other consideration must give way before this central and astounding fact. Implicit in that statement is our need – what we were, and what we were saved from. That, in itself, should be sufficient to secure our loyalty, but Paul's focus is much higher. His emphasis is not so much on what we have been saved from, but on what we have been saved for. God, Who has saved us, has 'called us with an holy calling'. Salvation is just the beginning – it brings us into a calling to holiness. It is that holiness – and the distinctiveness that it imparts – that makes persecution so likely, but we cannot abandon it for the sake of an easier life. It is part of God's plan for us.

The scale and significance of that plan are impossible to overstate. To communicate how remarkable it is, Paul points us to its roots and its revelation. Our salvation had its origins in God's 'purpose and grace' before the world began. 'His own purpose and grace' is a hendiadys – a figure of speech used for emphasis where, instead of using an adjective and a noun, two nouns joined by 'and' are used. The force of the expression here is 'His own gracious purpose.' That God should have an eternal purpose which involves us is remarkable. That this Divine purpose should be a purpose of grace is astounding, and should move us to such thanksgiving that shame should seem impossible.

Verse 10 What is true of the roots of this great message is true, too, of its revelation. Each of the Pastoral Epistles deals with the subject of revelation. 1 Timothy speaks of the revelation of an eternal Person, the One Who is the 'mystery of godliness,' a fitting example for the 'man of God' (1 Tim. 6:11). Writing to Titus, against the background of Cretan society and its proverbial disregard for the truth, Paul stresses the revelation of an eternal promise from the lips of God Who cannot lie (Tit. 1:1, 2). Now, as he appeared to be nothing more than insignificant flotsam, buffeted by the waves of Roman power, Paul rejoices in an eternal purpose far above and beyond the puny power of Caesar, a purpose that had been dramatically revealed in human history 'by the appearing of our Saviour Jesus Christ, who hath abolished death, and hath brought life and immortality to light through the gospel'. The figure is striking. Like an enormous floodlight, the appearing of the Lord Jesus has poured illumination on subjects that had been previously shrouded in shadow. Old Testament references to resurrection and immortality had been few and, on the whole, rather obscure. Now the darkness is dispelled and all of the glorious detail of the gospel exposed. It does not take too great an exertion of the imagination to imagine the dark and gloomy setting in which Paul penned these words. It requires a rather greater one to grasp how unspeakably precious they must have seemed to him. Physically, darkness and death pressed in, but spiritually Paul was basking in the brightness of Divine grace. 'The appearing of our Saviour Jesus Christ' refers to His first advent in the broadest sense, encompassing the incarnation and resurrection of the Lord Jesus and everything in between (*cf.* Tit. 2:11; 3:4).

These verses make up one of the three great salvation passages in the Pastoral Epistles. As we have seen, they stress the purpose of God in relation to our salvation. 1 Timothy 2:3–7 is another of these passages, and stresses the provision of Christ for salvation – He 'gave Himself a ransom for all'. Titus 3:5, the third of these passages stresses the power of the Holy Spirit in relation to salvation – 'He saved us, by the washing of regeneration, and renewing of the Holy Ghost.'

Verse 11 The 'testimony of our Lord', then, is not a message of which Timothy should feel ashamed. It follows that he should also not be ashamed of Paul, who was closely identified with the message: 'Whereunto I am appointed a preacher, and an apostle, and a teacher of the Gentiles'. Shackled in the gloom of Rome's death row, Paul was a pitiful figure, but not a shameful one. He still had an authority and a dignity that came, not from his upbringing, education, or intellect, but from his identification with the Gospel.

'Preacher' is *kēryx*, the word used for the herald and it is striking that here, as in 1 Timothy 2:7, 'preacher' precedes apostle – Paul is describing his activity before addressing his authority. The explanation, in this instance at least, may lie in the fact that Paul is presenting himself as a pattern for Timothy to follow and, while Timothy did not share in his apostolic appointment, he was called to be both a preacher and a teacher.

Paul's use of the term herald is replete with significance. The ancient herald was responsible to proclaim the message that he had been given clearly and faithfully. The message did not originate with him, he proclaimed it on the behalf of someone else. His task would be impossible if he was ashamed of his message, for it was not something to be whispered or mumbled, but an announcement to be cried at the top of his voice. Paul's responsibility, and Timothy's, was to do the very same thing with the message that they had received.

Paul's authority went beyond that of the herald, for he was also an apostle. He had already stressed his apostleship in the salutation to the epistle, and repeated here, it emphasises the closeness of the relationship between Paul and the message – to be ashamed of one was to be ashamed of the other. Finally, he identifies himself as a teacher of the gospel. While the gifts of the evangelist and the teacher are distinct from each other, we should be careful not to dichotomise too sharply between preaching and teaching. After all, God wills all men 'to be saved, and to come unto the knowledge of the truth' (1 Tim. 2:4). The KJV reading – a 'teacher of the

Gentiles' – points to Paul's unique dispensational role, but the stronger manuscript evidence supports the reading 'teacher', without defining his audience.

'Although all shall be offended', Peter had boasted, 'yet will not I.' Events, tragically, proved Him wrong. Paul must have faced the same temptation many times – keep low, stay quiet, moderate the message. We have all felt that temptation, and few of us would deny that there have been times when we yielded to it. For some of us, tragically, it has become our normal manner of life. May the words of the indomitable apostle convict our hearts and stir our souls, as we hear him exclaim, from the Stygian depths of a Roman dungeon: 'I am not ashamed: for I know whom I have believed!'

> *Jesus, and shall it ever be,*
> *A mortal man, ashamed of Thee?*
> *Ashamed of Thee, whom angels praise,*
> *Whose glories shine through endless days?*
> *Ashamed of Jesus! sooner far*
> *Let night disown each radiant star!*
> *'Tis midnight with my soul, till He,*
> *Bright morning star, bid darkness flee.*
> –Joseph Grigg

Verse 12 'I ... suffer these things'. The words are eloquent in their understatement. 'These things' included the physical privations of the Mamertine prison, the chafing of chains, the darkness, the hunger, the filth, and the abuse of inmates and custodians alike. It meant desertion and betrayal by those who had been friends, and intense loneliness and isolation. It meant the pressure of a looming trial and, beyond that, the virtual certainty of death. But, notwithstanding the range and the reality of his sufferings, Paul can say, not arrogantly or brashly, but as a statement of fact 'nevertheless I am not ashamed'.

In verse 8 Paul had exhorted Timothy not to be ashamed of 'the testimony of our Lord, nor of me His prisoner'. He offers himself here as a model of unashamed commitment to the message and, in verses 16–18, will present Onesiphorus as an example of unabashed loyalty to the messenger.

Paul is not ashamed of his imprisonment, his sufferings, nor of the message for which he suffers. That lack of shame was not an artefact of a strong personality, a thick skin, or ideological fanaticism. If that were the case, Paul's example would have little to say to the more timorous and retiring Timothy. But Paul's confidence arises, not from who he is, but from Whom he has trusted. He knows Whom he has believed, and his confidence in God dispels any shame that he might feel. And, therefore, his example is relevant to Timothy, who has put 'unfeigned faith' (v.5) in the very same God. Daniel's words were still true in Paul's day, as they are in ours: 'the people that do know their God shall be strong, and do exploits' (Dan. 11:32). As he suffered 'these things', it was Paul's knowledge of, and confidence in, God that allowed him to triumph. Paul's confidence in God's character gave him a corresponding confidence in His capability. He was 'persuaded' – that is, convinced by overwhelming arguments[19] – of God's ability to 'keep that which I have committed unto Him against that day'.

What is 'that which I have committed unto Him'? Many readers of this passage have seen in the expression a reference to Paul's soul and have found in the verse a ringing declaration of eternal security – a view movingly

---

[19] The same word is used of Paul's confidence in the reality of Timothy's conversion in 1:5. The perfect passive, used in both occurrences, 'expresses conviction of certainty' –Towner, *Timothy*, 454.

expressed by Daniel Whittle in his lovely hymn 'I know not why God's wondrous grace'. Others have understood the expression to refer to Paul's life of service, committed by him to God and sure to be rewarded in 'that day'. Yet others have seen both Paul's soul and his service in the verse. Both of these things are, of course, true. God would safely guard the apostle's soul to and through eternity. Paul could leave his service with the Lord, knowing that what he had done for God would be recognized and rewarded at the judgement seat of Christ. This understanding of the verse is reflected in the translation of the passage in a number of versions, including *KJV*, *NIV*, *ASV*, and *JND*. However, the translation of the clause in other versions, such as the *NET* and the *ESV* seems quite different. The *ESV*, for instance, renders it as follows: 'He is able to guard until that day what has been entrusted to me', a rendering which seems to point in exactly the opposite direction to the older versions.

The reason for the disagreement lies in the fact that the phrase 'that which I have committed unto Him' translates a single Greek word, *parathḗkē*, which means 'a deposit', and which was used to describe items of great value and importance that were entrusted to another for safekeeping. So, literally, Paul is confident that God is 'able to keep my deposit', and we must decide who has made this deposit, and with whom it has been made. We are helped to answer this question by observing that Paul uses the same word (or a very similar one) in 1 Timothy 6:20 ('that which is committed to thy trust') and in 2 Timothy 1:14 ('that ... which was committed unto thee'). In both of these passages the deposit is something that has been entrusted to Timothy and, in both of these passages, the deposit is apostolic teaching. That makes it likely that the same thing is in view in this verse, especially given the immediate context in this chapter.

Some commentators have suggested that there is a difficulty with Paul using the expression 'my deposit' to describe what God had entrusted to him – such a deposit, they argue, would surely be God's, not Paul's. And their argument is not without force – none of us would describe the savings that we have entrusted to the bank as being the bank's deposit; we would be quite emphatic that it was ours. Moreover, it can be argued that 'since it is God who is here envisioned as guarding 'my deposit', the idiom demands that it is therefore something entrusted *to* God ... not something that God has entrusted to another that he yet continues to guard'.[20]

There is a simple solution to these difficulties that allows *paratheke* to be understood in a way that is consistent with the two other occasions when Paul uses it. Paul is not speaking of that which he has committed to God. Nor is he speaking of that which God has committed to him. Rather, he is referring to what he has committed to Timothy – what he describes in the following verse as 'the form of sound words, which thou hast heard of me'. This is why it is *his* deposit – although he did receive it from God in the first instance, the point here is that he has now entrusted it to Timothy. The fact that it is God Who is able to guard this deposit is a comfort and a reassurance not only to the apostle, who must now entrust his life's work to another, but to Timothy who is being reminded once again of one of the great themes of this chapter – that he is responsible to be faithful in his service for God, but that he only can do so with Divine enablement. Paul was depending on Timothy, but his confidence was not so much in

---

[20] Fee, *1 & 2 Timothy*, 232.

Timothy as in the God whom they had both believed and who was – and is – able to guard the precious deposit of apostolic truth 'against that day'.

'That day' takes our minds forward to the end of the dispensation – to the Rapture and the events that follow it. On that day, the burden of testimony will at last be laid down, and the faithfulness of the servants who carried it – from the apostle onwards – will be finally and fairly assessed. As Paul contemplated 'that day', the apparent importance of 'these things' fell away. Glory then meant that shame had no place now, for Paul was on the winning side, even if the victory would come only at the end of a long and arduous conflict.

The preservation of the deposit for which Paul trusted God was not just a matter of a couple of generations, or even a few centuries. Nor was it possible that the deposit would be preserved for most of the dispensation, only to be let slip in its closing days. Right on to the end, to the glory of 'that day', God would preserve this precious deposit.

The balance of Divine power and human responsibility in this chapter and in this verse ought to challenge and comfort us. Our faithfulness to God and His Word matters. We cannot lightly esteem or carelessly handle the deposit that we have received. The safeguarding of so precious a burden demands our utmost. But let us never think that the burden rests on our shoulders alone. As we look back over the centuries of Christian testimony, we thank God that He has preserved his truth amidst opposition that at times seemed insurmountable. We thank Him for those faithful men and women of God – not just the heroes and heroines of biographies, but those ordinary, unnamed believers who refused to be ashamed. But as we do so, we give thanks, above all, for the God Who is able and Who, behind the scenes and through His servants, has preserved His precious Truth.

Verse 13 A similar balance between Divine and human responsibility is seen in verses 13 and 14. In each verse there is an imperative verb: 'hold fast' (v. 13) and 'keep' (v. 14). Severally and collectively, they call Timothy to action. But, once again, he is spared from any thought of self-reliance – he is to keep the deposit 'by the Holy Ghost which dwelleth in us'. Timothy must 'hold fast the form of sound words, which thou hast heard of me'. While newer translations tend to render this expression as 'retain' or 'hold', there is a great deal to be said for the KJV's 'hold fast'.[21] That expression, while perhaps a trifle dated, is appropriately striking in its force. Timothy must cling tenaciously to what he has received from the apostle. However we translate the word, implicit in it is the idea of holding onto what one has already taken hold of. This is an obvious point, but one whose importance it would be difficult to overstate. We cannot guard what we have not grasped, and it is vital that we lay hold of Scripture for ourselves. This is vital, not just for our own individual Christian lives, but for the blessing of God's people and the progress of God's work. To be a man or woman of God will require making the Word of God our own personal possession and, once we have laid hold on it, hanging on with all our strength.

'The form of sound words, which thou hast heard of me' offers another description of the deposit mentioned in verses 12 and 14 – they are substantively identical. The expression embraces the teaching of the apostle. 'Form' is *hypotypōis*. This can mean 'an outline, sketch, [or] brief

---

[21] The ESV's 'follow' is, lexically, contextually, and stylistically, a particularly poor choice of translation.

and summary exposition',[22] but Paul is not speaking here of a sketchy outline that Timothy is to elaborate at will. Rather, he is using the word in the sense of 'a model, form, or standard'.[23] Paul uses the same word in a different context, but with a similar meaning in 1 Timothy 1:16: 'a pattern to them which should hereafter believe'. The form is not a sketch to be elaborated, but a standard to be maintained. It is not insignificant that Paul refers to the 'standard of words'. This calls for fidelity, not just to Paul's ideas or concepts, but to the words that the apostle had deposited with Timothy.

The standard to which Timothy must adhere is validated in two ways: by its soundness and its source. The adjective 'sound' (*hygiainō*) is one of the distinctive words of the Pastoral Epistles (see 1 Tim. 1:10, 6:3; 2 Tim. 1:13, 4:3; Tit. 1:9, 13, 2:1, 2), but its uses outside of the pastorals are instructive. On three occasions, Dr Luke will use the term to describe perfect physical health (5:31, 7:10, 15:27), and John uses the word in a similar way in 3 John 1:2. The emphasis in the Pastorals is upon doctrinal healthfulness. In contrast to the diseased and corrupting teaching of false teachers like Hymenaeus and Philetus, whose word eats 'as a canker' (2 Tim. 2:17), the teaching of the apostle was healthy, producing robust Christianity and uncontaminated godliness.[24]

The standard, then, is validated by its soundness, but also by its source: 'which thou hast heard of me'. Apostolic authority mattered. Paul will develop this idea

---

[22] Thayer, *s.v.*
[23] Towner, *Timothy*, 477.
[24] *Hygiainō* is the word from which we get 'hygiene'. As always in these cases, we should be careful about reading too much of the new word's meaning back into the older word. In this case, hygiene's meaning 'free from contamination' short-changes the positive implications of *hygiainō*. For a useful discussion of the dangers of this sort of 'semantic anachronism' see D.A. Carson, *Exegetical Fallacies* (2nd ed.), (Carlisle: Paternoster, 1996), 33–35.

in chapter 2 of this epistle – Timothy can be sure about the authenticity of the teaching that he has received because it has come to him directly from the apostle. And so can we. While we can no longer listen to the voice of the apostle, we still have the 'the form of sound words, which thou hast heard of me'. While we cannot hear the words, we can read them, for on the pages of the New Testament we have the teaching of the apostles, with all of the authenticity and all of the authority that it had for Timothy. The deposit has arrived in our hands, and it is still our task to hold it fast.

The remit of our task goes no wider than the 'form of sound words'. It is not tradition that we must hold fast, not philosophy, not psychology, not our favourite applications, but the sound words of apostolic teaching. We can easily spend our time mastering subjects that are related to Scripture, and that may illuminate and enhance our understanding of the Word of God. These studies may be useful, and have their place, but we must ever be careful that our priority is to lay hold, for ourselves, on the teaching of Scripture, for only thus will we be able to hold fast the form of sound words.

What we hold matters, but it also matters how we hold it – 'in faith and love which is in Christ Jesus'. An ideology can be maintained for a very long time by means of a fervent fanaticism. But it is not to this that Timothy is called, any more than he is expected to hold fast the truth in a detached and academic fashion. Rather, he must do so in constant and conscious dependence on Christ and in both the enjoyment of Christ's love to him and the expression of that love towards others.

Verse 14 'Guard the good deposit entrusted to you' (ESV). The verb 'guard' means to preserve against loss or damage, and is in the aorist imperative, conveying a sense of urgency, underscored by the repetition of an instruction so similar in force to that of verse 13. It is used 'of guarding a palace against marauders and possessions against thieves (Lk. 11:21; Acts 22:20)' and stresses the hostile environment in which and in spite of which truth must be preserved.[25] 'Good' (*kalos*) parallels 'sound' in the previous verse and is likewise a word that is especially associated with the Pastoral Epistles. Out of 102 occurrences in the New Testament, twenty-two are found in the Pastoral Epistles, most often as 'good works'. The word has the idea of the external manifestation of essential excellence – it means both beautiful and good. It is a fitting description of the gospel, and another reminder to Timothy that this is not a message to be ashamed of, for to be good is the antithesis of being shameful.

This guarding is to be done 'by the Holy Ghost which dwelleth in us'. In referring to the Holy Spirit, Paul is continuing the theme of Divine enablement. His reference to the Holy Spirit echoes verse 7, and the two verses form an *inclusio* bracketing the section, emphasising the importance of this theme. The fact that the Holy Spirit is described as 'dwelling in us' is a lovely underscoring of the intertwining of human responsibility and Divine resource that has run through the chapter. The Holy Spirit is seen working in and through human agents, enabling them to do what, in their own strength, they could not hope to achieve.

Paul's use of the plural – 'us' – is equally precious. In the immediate context, it binds Paul and Timothy together, and assures Timothy that Paul had no secret and special reserve of strength that is unavailable to him. Paul was handing over a ministry to Timothy, but not the

---

[25] Stott, *2 Timothy*, 44.

power for the ministry, because it was not his to give, and because Timothy already had it. And it furnishes us with the same assurance, for there is no reason to limit the scope of 'us' to Paul and Timothy. It embraces all believers, for every one of us has the Holy Ghost dwelling in us, equipping us for the same task with the same inexhaustible power.

vv. 15–18   Exemplified

Verses 8 to 14 of this chapter deal with Timothy's attitude to Paul and to the gospel at a time when association with the messenger or his message involved opprobrium and shame, and significant danger. Against this background, Paul exhorted Timothy 'Be not thou therefore ashamed of the testimony of our Lord, nor of me his prisoner' (v. 8). In the closing section of the chapter, he underlines his exhortation by presenting Timothy with two examples, one negative and one positive.

Verse 15 presents the negative example: 'all they which are in Asia be turned away from me'. We should not dismiss this as the self-pitying exaggeration of a depressed old man. Later in the epistle, Paul spells out just what this betrayal had meant for him: 'At my first answer no man stood with me, but all men forsook me' (2 Tim. 4:16). Paul stood alone before Nero. Not one of the believers in Asia – to whom Paul had preached, who he had seen saved, with whom he had prayed, and laboured, and whom he loved – stood with him. There is no suggestion here that they had turned aside from sound doctrine – likely their belief remained irreproachably orthodox. But, when Paul had become an embarrassment, when association with the apostle entailed shame and danger, they had all melted away, leaving him isolated and lonely at his hour of greatest need.

In the world of the unsaved, this is nothing remarkable. No matter how popular or influential an individual is, as soon as they become a liability, the cord is cut, the calls go unreturned, and, as much as possible, the embarrassing friend or colleague is airbrushed from memory. We can expect no more of the world. But we should expect more of believers, and we should expect more from ourselves. Paul did, and we catch something of the bitterness on his disappointment in this verse.

From amongst 'all they which are in Asia', he singles out two: Phygellus and Hermogenes. We know nothing of these two men, except their names. There is a deep irony in this. Concern for their own reputation led them to be ashamed of the apostle. The act of betrayal that this concern prompted ensured that their names would live on in infamy. Paul's reference to 'that day' in verse 12 has already reminded us of the importance of a long-term view, and he will repeat the phrase and its emphasis in verse 18. The example of Phygellus and Hermogenes should likewise encourage us to think of the long-term – the eternal – consequences of our choices and our actions.

Verses 16–18 It is with a sense of relief that we turn from Phygellus and Hermogenes to the very different example provided by Onesiphorus. Onesiphorus's name means 'bringing profit', and he abundantly lived up to it. He 'oft refreshed' Paul. Our efforts to imagine the conditions of Paul's incarceration must surely fall short of the reality, and it is correspondingly difficult for us to imagine just how, and in how many ways, the apostle was refreshed by the visits of this steadfast brother who 'was not ashamed of my chain'. So far from being ashamed, Onesiphorus sought Paul out as soon as he arrived in Rome. The difficulties and dangers involved in that search must have been considerable. Certainly, it involved something more than just bureaucratic inconvenience. To traipse the streets of Rome asking official after official about the whereabouts of a prominent prisoner being held on a capital charge would not have been a comfortable business. Onesiphorus might have been forgiven for quietly finishing his business in Rome and slipping off home without making any such efforts. But that was not the character of the man, and he did seek Paul out 'very diligently' – the word has both the sense of 'earnestly' and 'at the earliest opportunity'[26] – and having found him visited him again and again. This faithfulness to the apostle was nothing new for Onesiphorus, for Paul could remind Timothy of 'how many things he ministered unto me at Ephesus'. Onesiphorus was that most lovely of things, a consistent Christian, whose loyalty did not ebb and flow with circumstances, but who could be relied on to be helpfully and wholeheartedly present even when the going got tough.

It seems likely that Onesiphorus had concluded his business in Rome by the time that Paul writes. It may be that Paul's reference in verse 16 to 'the house of Onesiphorus' indicates that he was absent from home. This is not inevitable, though, as the expression could include Onesiphorus, just as Paul's references to 'the house of Stephanas' in 1 Corinthians seem likely to include Stephanas himself.[27] Certainly, there is no basis in the passage for assuming that Onesiphorus had died.

---

[26] Thayer, *Greek Lexicon*, s.v. The NET's rendering of the word as 'eagerly' nicely captures its sense. The KJV's 'when he was in Rome' could also be translated 'when he arrived in Rome' (see, for example, ESV, NKJV, NET), which further emphasises the priority that Onesiphorus gave to refreshing Paul.

[27] 1 Corinthians 1:16; 16:15, 17. See the discussion in Towner, *Timothy*, 482, 483 and Mounce, *Pastoral Epistles*, 494–497.

That assumption is usually made as a preliminary to arguing that Paul's prayer in verse 18 must therefore be an example of prayer for the dead. In response to this it is probably only necessary to observe that any doctrine that relies on such desperate exegetical expedients is not to be taken very seriously.

What is noteworthy about Paul's reference to 'the house of Onesiphorus' is that it indicates that Onesiphorus was a man of some means and social standing. The man who sought out Paul so eagerly was not someone who had nothing to lose. He had a family, and he had property, and this compounded the risk that he was taking in his identification with Paul, but he did not allow that to stop him.

Paul prays for mercy for this household. Whether there were specific and immediate circumstances that prompted that prayer, we cannot say without venturing into speculation. For whatever reason, Paul felt that they needed 'the kind of help that is a necessity and only the Lord can give' and he prays that they will receive what they need, and that Onesiphorus' selfless succouring of the apostle will be recompensed by God.[28]

Paul's sense of gratitude to and appreciation of Onesiphorus is so strong that, having commenced to speak about him with the prayer wish of verse 16, he closes his recollections with another prayer: 'The Lord grant unto him that he may find mercy of the Lord in that day'. Only the most wishful thinking could distort this into a prayer for the salvation of a dead man. Not only is there no basis for assuming that Onesiphorus is dead; Paul is not praying for his salvation. Rather, in his characteristic way, Paul is looking on to 'that day'. This is the same day mentioned in verse 12, and it is the judgement seat of Christ that Paul has particularly in

---

[28] Towner, *Timothy*, 482.

mind here. Paul's play on words makes it clear that his prayer is for Onesiphorus' faithful dedication to be rewarded at the *bema* – he found Paul (v. 17) and Paul asks that he will find mercy (v. 18) in that day. Onesiphorus' loyalty to Paul will have eternal consequences.

Summary Paul opened this epistle by reminding Timothy of the close relationship that existed between them. This provided the basis for the charge to Timothy that occupies the rest of the epistle – it is not just the charge of a teacher to a disciple, but of a father to a son. Paul also reminds Timothy of a venerable heritage, stretching back beyond the immediately preceding generations to include the whole sweep of the Divine programme. Timothy has become part of an awfully big plan, and has a responsibility to play his part in the progress of that plan. Paul reminds him that he has been equipped for this responsibility. The gift that he has received (v. 6) and the impartation of the 'Spirit of power, and of love, and of a sound mind' (v. 7) provide Timothy with the resources that he needs to discharge his responsibility. That responsibility is clearly spelled out: 'Be not thou therefore ashamed of the testimony of our Lord, nor of me his prisoner' (v. 8). Paul urged Timothy to guard and keep the deposit of Divine truth, 'the form of sound words' (v. 13) that he has received and drives his exhortation home with a pair of examples – one that Timothy must eschew, and another that he should emulate.

Chapter Two

2:1–13 The anticipation of the man of God

vv. 1–7   Service and the Future

There is a distinct shift in focus as we move to chapter 2. Chapter 1, as we have seen, was largely occupied with the past – with Timothy's past, Paul's past, and the long unfolding history of Divine purpose. Timothy's present was to be informed by all that lay in the past. As we move into chapter 2, our attention is turned to the future. Timothy's life in the present was to be shaped, not just by his appreciation of the past, but by his expectation of the future. So it is for us – it is important that we keep our eye on both the past – on what God has done in human history and in our own lives – and on the future. It is easy for us to become unbalanced, to live so much in the past or (perhaps less often) the future that we lose sight of the importance and urgency of serving God in the present. Like Timothy, we need to heed the call to action that Paul gives at the commencement of this chapter.

Verse 1 opens with 'thou therefore', one of the expressions that is a significant feature of this epistle. At the end of chapter 1, Paul had been speaking about individuals who serve as examples – and counter-examples – of faithfulness and commitment. But now the spotlight turns squarely on Timothy. He is to learn from the examples presented, but not to become occupied with them, for what matters for Timothy is not how others have behaved, but how faithful he has been. This forceful 'but you' turns the focus from the failures of others to Timothy's responsibility. Before he addresses that responsibility, however, he directs Timothy to the resource that will empower him for it: 'Thou therefore, my son, be strong in the grace that is in Christ Jesus'.

'Be strong' is literally 'be empowered'. It is a passive verb – Paul is not exhorting Timothy to dig deep within himself for innate resources of courage to meet the difficulties that he faces. Rather, he is to avail of a provision that is made for him – to allow God to empower him. This is no ordinary provision. 'Empower' picks up on the references to Divine power in the first chapter of the epistle: in the 'Spirit of power' of verse 7 and 'He is able' [literally 'powerful'] of verse 12. So, for the challenges of service, Timothy is to be empowered, not with any arsenal of human assistance, but with the power of God, imparted to him by the Spirit of God.

Timothy is to 'be strong in the grace that is in Christ Jesus'. While this expression could refer to grace as the location of Timothy's strength, it is more likely that it describes the means by which Timothy is empowered – 'be strengthened by the grace that is in Christ Jesus' (ESV). Divine power is communicated by Divine grace. Grace is not just an attribute of God, static and unchanging. Grace is God in action, moving to meet the need of sinner and of saint. It is dynamic and enabling, and nothing else could meet Timothy's need – or ours. And this grace is found, as God's grace always is, 'in Christ Jesus'.

Everyone in Asia had turned away from Paul. If they had turned from him they would turn from Timothy too. As he sought carry out the mandate of this epistle he would frequently find himself isolated and lonely. But he was not alone – the three persons of the Trinity were joined in empowering him – the Spirit of power [*dynamis*] (1:7), God Who is 'able' [*dynatos*] (1:12), and Christ Jesus, in Whom is found the supply of grace to empower [*endynamoō*] him in his service for God. It was this power – and only this power – that would equip Timothy to 'commit' the truth to faithful men (2:2) and to 'endure hardness' (2:3).

Verse 2 Apostolic succession was one of the hotly contested issues of the Reformation. In general, this term refers to the belief that Papal and priestly power has been transferred by the laying of hands from generation to generation ever since the time of the apostles. A number of the denominations of Christendom still claim that their authority and authenticity derives from this link with the apostles. This concept of apostolic succession owes more to men's imagination than it does to the Scriptures. By contrast, this verse outlines the apostolic succession that really matters: not the tenuous transmission of apostolic influence through the ages, but the clear communication of apostolic teaching from generation to generation – from Paul to Timothy to 'faithful men' to 'others also', and to others, and others, and others right down to our present day. Timothy's service looks beyond his generation, and his faithfulness would ultimately impact many generations to come. The same is true of our service. We do not know when Christ will return or for how much longer the present age of testimony will continue. But we do well to remember that, just as we have been faithfully taught the Word of God by a generation that is now departed or departing, so we have a responsibility to faithfully communicate that truth to a new generation of believers.

It is vital that this process happens without 'generation loss'. This is a concept that will be familiar to those of us who were raised in a pre-digital world, where lossless copying was impossible. We have had the experience of trying to decipher the faded print on a photocopy of a photocopy of a photocopy, with all the accumulated imperfections of 'lossy transmission'. And even those of more recent vintage may have played the game formerly known as 'Chinese Whispers', where a message is whispered along the line of players, gathering a (hopefully amusing) cargo of transmission errors along the way. What would be amusing in the playground or mildly frustrating in the classroom would be extremely serious, and potentially disastrous for the transmission of Divine truth, and so Paul stresses the importance of maintaining the integrity of truth as it is transmitted.

It is for this reason that he emphasises that Timothy must communicate 'the things that thou hast heard of me among many witnesses'. Notwithstanding the intimacy of the relationship between Paul and Timothy, the apostle had taken care to ensure that he had taught Timothy publicly 'among many witnesses'. This would have made it impossible for Timothy to pass off as authentically Pauline and apostolic some teaching that he had invented or imagined for himself. If he deviated in any way from the apostolic doctrine any number of brethren could have stepped forward and said 'that's not what Paul said'. What was wise in Paul's day is still wise in ours – truth should be taught publicly and openly. Doctrine that must be whispered covertly and that cannot be openly taught in the assembly is unlikely to be the apostles' doctrine, and should be avoided. Paul had already taught Timothy that the local church is 'the pillar and ground of the truth' (1 Tim. 3:15), and it is still the place where God intends truth to be transmitted.

What Timothy taught was not just to be compatible with, or based upon, what the apostle had taught him. Rather, it was to be 'the same' – identical in content to that which he had received. There is no thought here of a doctrinal trajectory, begun by Paul, and developed by Timothy and succeeding generations. The truth that Timothy was to transmit was static and unchanging. Today, we are still required to teach 'the same' truth – not elaborating or embroidering, not trimming or tweaking, but communicating the same truth that Paul delivered and that Timothy received and taught to 'faithful men'.

Truth was to be committed or entrusted – Paul used the verb form of the noun 'deposit' (*cf.* 1:14, 1 Tim. 6:20). There would be nothing casual or haphazard about this handover. Truth would be passed with care and with clarity to the faithful men; men who could be trusted. It is clear from 4:2 that Timothy was to preach to everyone and anyone. But he was to take particular care to commit the truth to faithful men. We know nothing about these men – who they were, what they were called, and what they looked like have long been forgotten. But we know that they were faithful, for the truth committed to them was not committed in vain. We owe an incalculable amount to these nameless, faceless, faithful men.

Faithful men are still needed. Down through the generations the precious deposit has come, until it has landed at last in our hands. In the following verses, we will discover that what we do with this trust will have enormous and eternal implications for us. But that is not, or should not be, our only motive for faithfulness. What we do with Divine truth will affect generations still unborn. May we not fail them, or fail God, but let us faithfully play our part in the real apostolic succession.

Verses 3–6 The focus on the future intensifies in the sequence of metaphors that Paul uses in verses 4–6 – the soldier (v. 4), the athlete (v. 5), and the farmer (v. 6).[1] These are introduced by the soldier simile in verse 3, which is distinct from the three pictures that follow it. With its introduction of the theme of suffering, this overarching exhortation to Timothy acts as a pivot to the theme of future reward, which is the common thread uniting the three metaphors that follow.

Verse 3 Paul exhorts Timothy to 'take thy share in suffering as a good soldier of Jesus Christ' (JND). The word for 'hardness' is a distinctive word of this epistle (it occurs here, 2:9, 4:5, and elsewhere only in James 5:13). It occurs here with a prefix that indicates a suffering together.[2] A number of translations suggest that Paul is calling on Timothy to share in his sufferings.[3] While there is little doubt that that is true, there is no need to narrow the scope of Paul's exhortation in this way. Timothy is to co-suffer not only with the apostle, but with all who, then and later, will seek to be faithful stewards of the Word of God. He did not stand alone, for he was part of a vast army of suffering soldier-stewards. This co-suffering will reveal Timothy to be a 'good soldier'. The nuances of the adjective 'good' (*kalos*) include genuine, worthy, and approved. Timothy's willingness to suffer will approve him as a soldier of

---

[1] Paul uses a similar sequence of metaphors in 1 Corinthians 9:7,8, 24–27. However, it is important to notice that he uses them there in quite a different way, to make a different point.

[2] A number of MSS (which are followed by the Textus Receptus, KJV and NKJV) repeat 'thou therefore' at the beginning of verse 3, and omit the prefix to the word for suffering. See Bruce M. Metzger, *A Textual Commentary on the Greek New Testament* 2nd edition, (Stuttgart: Deutsche Bibel Gesellschaft, 1994), 579.

[3] E.g. NIV: 'Join with me in suffering'.

Christ Jesus – it will 'distinguish the outstanding soldier ("good") from the mediocre.'[4]

The idea of suffering becomes the pivot that turns the focus of the chapter to the future. Or, to put it another way, the verses that follow this injunction are all intended to answer the question 'why suffer?' For the Christian, there is always an answer to that question, and it always, ultimately, lies in the future. Timothy will suffer because he stewards, but he stewards because of the future. Faithfulness now means hardship now, but faithfulness now means reward then. This is vital truth that is emphasised in the pictures that follow.

Verse 4 Soldiers need to be tough: they must be prepared to suffer. In this verse Paul emphasises another characteristic of the soldier – single-minded dedication to his duty. This soldier is not on standby in the barracks, but is on active service: Paul's use of the present participle 'warreth' emphasises that he is presently in the battle. In those moments the soldier has no time to be distracted by the mundane details of civilian life.

The word 'entangle' occurs on one other occasion in the New Testament (2 Pet. 2:20), where it is used of being entangled in 'the pollutions of the world'. Outside of the New Testament, it is used to describe 'a sheep or hare being tangled in thorns'.[5] 'The affairs of this life' are not sinful (or at least not necessarily so) but nonetheless they have the potential to 'entangle' the soldier, hampering and hindering his usefulness in the battle, and compromising his ability to please the 'one who has enlisted him as a soldier' (*JND*).

---

[4] Towner, *Timothy*, 492.
[5] Mounce, *Pastoral Epistles*, 509.

The soldier's motivation is striking. It is not so much to win the battle. Nor is it to secure promotion through the ranks or acquire a chestful of medals. His motivation is to please his commander. In doing so, he will do his utmost to ensure that the battle is not lost. A consequence of his doing so will be recognition of and recompense for his dedicated service. But his true motivation is both simpler and more profound – it is the pleasure of his commander.

This verse has challenging practical implications for us. We are – or we should be – conscious of the danger to our spiritual development and usefulness posed by things that are dirty and defiling. We are far less concerned – and far less concerned than we should be – about things that are distracting: the ensnaring details of our ordinary, everyday life that so easily divert us from the only goal that really matters – the pleasure of the One who has enlisted us as soldiers.

Verse 5 Paul turns to the domain of athletics in verse 5, from the dedication of the soldier to the diligence of the athlete. In doing so, he leaves no room for the supposition that zeal is all that matters, or that dedication to a cause is sufficient to excuse any approach that we might adopt. In spiritual things, the end does not justify the means, and no amount of zeal, determination, or commitment can change that.

Paul introduces us to an athlete who is 'striving for masteries'. The whole expression translates the familiar looking verb *athleō*, and catches the word's connotations of effort and competition. There is nothing relaxed or casual about this competitor. The image here is of an athlete who is in it to win it, who is straining every nerve, and bone, and sinew to win the race, and gain the prize. But, no matter how badly that athlete wants to win the race and wear the victor's crown, he or she must compete by the rules, must 'strive lawfully'. Any other approach can only result in disqualification and disappointment.

In the context of the competitions that Paul is drawing upon for his imagery, 'striving lawfully' embraced more than just the period between the report of the starter's pistol and crossing the finish line. Competitors in the Greek games were required to complete a programme of disciplined training for ten months before they were qualified to compete at all.[6] For that period of ten months, every aspect of their lives would be governed by the future prospect of winning the crown. Every decision, every action, every moment would have to be lived with the prospect of future glory in mind. And, as Paul says as he uses similar imagery in 1 Corinthians, if 'they do it to obtain a corruptible crown'(1 Cor. 9:25), how much more ought we, who seek one that is uncorruptible.

This is a principle that can, and should, be applied to every area of our Christian life. It is not unusual to hear practices that are unscriptural excused because the person doing them 'loves the Lord' or is marked by zeal. Love for the Lord and zeal for His work are essential, and we could all do with more of them. But we cannot expect to be rewarded for our efforts and we cannot hope to please the Lord if we are not striving lawfully.

In the immediate context, 'striving lawfully' refers primarily to Timothy's faithfulness to the charge of the first two verses. He was to strive lawfully by his adherence to 'the things he had received' and he was to strive lawfully in communicating it to 'faithful men'. Above all, he was to strive lawfully in 'sharing in suffering'. He could avoid suffering, if he wanted to, but only by not striving lawfully. If he chose not to abide by

---

[6] See Marshall, *Pastoral Epistles*, 730 and Kelly, *Pastoral Epistles*, 175–177.

the rules, he could live in such a way that the suffering would go away. But if the suffering vanished, so would the crown – he could not have one without the other.

No more can we. Faithfulness to God still matters, and we are still called to devotion and diligence. May God grant us grace to serve Him undistractedly and obediently, as good soldiers of Christ Jesus.

Verse 6 Paul then shifts to the third figure: 'It is the hard-working farmer who ought to have the first share of the crops' (ESV). Some commentators have struggled to understand how this image relates to the first two, a confusion that is sometimes compounded by the view that this image, and that of the soldier in verse 4 relate here (as they do in 1 Corinthians 9) to the issue of support for the Lord's servants.[7] Notwithstanding the shared imagery, the emphasis of the two passages is very different, and while the issue of the proper material support of those who serve the Lord and His people is a very important one, it is altogether tangential to the concerns of this chapter. Rather, this picture recapitulates the same themes that we have seen in the two preceding pictures – firstly, the importance of living the present in the light of future reward, and secondly that the Christian life is a serious business, not to be lived casually and haphazardly but with exertion and effort and a willingness to 'suffer hardship' in the service of God.

It is, perhaps, worth noting that this verse states a principle. It outlines what is fitting and necessary – 'the hard working farmer *ought* to have first share of the

---

[7] See, for example, C.K. Barrett, *The Pastoral Epistles in the New English Bible*, (Oxford: Clarendon, 1963), 102; Martin Dibelius and Hans Conzelmann, *The Pastoral Epistles*, (Minneapolis, MN: Fortress Press, 1972), 108; Kelly, *Pastoral Epistles*, 175–177, and Robert W. Yarbrough, *The Letters to Timothy and Titus* The Pillar Bible Commentary, (London: Apollos, 2018), 375.

crops'.⁸ It is right and proper that the one who invested hard labour in the cultivation of the field, the planting of the seed and the fertilising, weeding and tending to the plants should get the first share of the resulting crop. Strenuous labour is involved. The language used has the idea of toil to the point of exhaustion. Having grown up on a farm I can testify (though more at second than first hand) to the fact that farm labour is taxing. It involves long hours and hard work. And it involves waiting. Long before the crop can be reaped, the ground must be tilled, and the seeds sown. There will be a significant period of waiting, for seeds to germinate, plants to grow, and crops to mature. But without the hard work, there will be no fruit. The early risings, and late nights, the aching backs and blistered palms all need to happen now, so that when the harvest comes, there is fruit to be gathered.

The applicability of this picture to our Christian experience should be clear. In this age of instant gratification, we are called upon to work hard for the future, without seeing immediate results, but in the knowledge that those results will follow. This has never been an easy thing to do, and the temper of our own age and society makes it perhaps especially difficult for us. But just as the farmer looks at the cold and unpromising blankness of a freshly sown field and knows that months hence he will reap a full harvest, so we, amongst the sufferings and setbacks of our Christian lives, can work hard, knowing that there will be fruit, in which we will have the first share. And let us not forget that Paul wrote these words in prison, in apparent failure, after a lifetime of the most diligent service possible to imagine. From the darkness of the prison, and the loneliness and

---

⁸ Darby gives a different emphasis to the verse: 'The husbandman must labour before partaking of the fruits'. That is true enough, but less in keeping with the thrust of Paul's argument here.

disappointment of desertion by his converts and friends, Paul looks confidently to the future, knowing that he will receive the first share of the fruit, in the reward that he would receive. If he could have such confidence surely we can too.

It is important to notice that Paul does not suggest that the hard working farmer will take all of the fruit. He gets the first share, a special portion for himself. 'First' stresses both the certainty of the crop and Timothy's priority in partaking of it. He partakes, rather than taking, for the blessing of the crop will be shared. Others will benefit from the farmer's hard work – a point that Paul will develop in verse 10.

The three images, then, have all insisted that we live in the present with the future in view, and that we balance present suffering, and present diligence against future, eschatological reward. 'Each links disciplined, diligent performance to obtaining a valuable goal. And as the pictures unfold, the concept of goal develops from the implicit to the explicit promise of reward.'[9] Indeed, the pictures provide us with a range of distinct, though linked, motivations: pleasing God (v. 4), winning the crown (v. 5), and receiving the first share of the fruits (v. 6). Severally and together, these are such prospects, such glorious goals, as should make any suffering pale and any exertion easy.

Verse 7 Paul draws the section to a close with a command and a promise. Timothy is to 'consider what I say'. This expression is 'a well known didactic formula' equivalent to 'pay attention or, in our modern vernacular, 'Listen up!''[10] It may also involve careful consideration of the contents of the preceding verses,

---

[9] Towner, *Timothy*, 495.
[10] Towner, *Timothy*, 496.

meaning something akin to 'work out what I am getting at'.[11] Whatever the precise nuance, the implication is the same. The instructions of verses 1–3 and the images of verses 4–6 demanded Timothy's close attention and careful consideration. They demand ours too, for they cut across the comfortable complacency of our own otiose existence, rebuking our casual Christianity and our lack of discipline and diligence. As we look to the future, we should fight, and run, and plant, and live our lives as though our faith was the only thing that mattered because, in the final analysis, nothing else does.

With the command comes a promise: 'the Lord will give you understanding in everything' (ESV).[12] This promise brings together a source, a supply, and a scope. The source is 'the Lord'. At the start of the chapter, we saw that Timothy was being empowered in 'the grace that is in Christ Jesus'. The One Who empowered Timothy in verse 1 is the same One Who enlightens him in this verse. He is not left to fall back upon his native intelligence or to rely on his own mental capabilities. He is, and we are, promised Divinely supplied insight and understanding. This is the supply in the verse. In the immediate context, this insight must have to do specifically with the wisdom to determine proper priorities, the insight that could look beyond the painfulness of the suffering to the glory of the reward, and order everyday life accordingly. But Paul widens the scope of the promise beyond these immediate concerns – Timothy can look to the Lord for enlightenment in 'everything' ('all things', JND).

We should notice the connection – and the balance – between the command and the promise. Timothy is to

---

[11] So Kelly, *Pastoral Epistles*, 177.
[12] The words are a promise, rather than the prayer that the KJV rendering might suggest ('the Lord give thee understanding in all things').

consider what Paul says, but his understanding will not ultimately come from his own cognition or powers of reasoning. The Lord will give him understanding but, by the same token, that understanding does not bypass or override Timothy's own considering, the deliberate and painstaking exercise of his intellectual capabilities. Though we would not want to lose sight of the meaning that these words had for Timothy in the specific context of this chapter, we might find in them a useful template for our own Bible study. We have a responsibility to consider, but we look dependently to God to give us understanding in all things.

vv. 8–10   Saints and the Future

2 Timothy 2:3 charges Timothy to 'endure hardness as a good soldier of Jesus Christ' – to suffer as a seasoned soldier should. This is followed by the picture of the soldier, the athlete, and the farmer. All three resound with a common implication. We should serve and strive and suffer now in the light of a reward that is to come.

In verses 8 and 9 of the chapter, which make up a single sentence in the original, Paul continues to answer the question 'why suffer?', and he continues to answer it by pointing Timothy to the future. But, from speaking in verses 4–7 about the future and its priorities, he addresses the future and its power. This is an important development in the apostle's argument. Motivating present privation, self-denial, and suffering only works if the reward is certain. The athlete only competes on this basis – he knows that there is a crown to be won. Similarly, the farmer only works hard because he knows that the laws of nature guarantee a coming harvest. Now Timothy is being urged to suffer in the prospect of coming glory. Is there any guarantee that, if he does suffer, glory will follow? It is this question that Paul addresses in these verses.

Verse 8 Paul begins with the imperative 'Remember'. It is not that Paul apprehends any real likelihood of Timothy's having forgotten these great and glorious facts about the Lord Jesus Christ, but rather that he wants him to have them in the forefront of his thinking. The verb is in the present tense – it has the force 'keep on remembering'. It is no surprise that Paul points Timothy to Christ. Time and again, in the New Testament, believers who are suffering are urged, in the words of the writer to the Hebrews to 'look stedfastly upon Jesus' (Heb. 12:2, JND), to 'consider Him that endured such contradiction of sinners against Himself' (Heb. 12:3). Christ, Peter tells us, 'suffered for us, leaving us an example that we should follow His steps' (1 Pet. 2:21). Now Paul, too, points Timothy to Christ.

It is not, however, the sufferings of Christ that Paul, in this context, wants Timothy to remember. To grasp what he has in mind, it is helpful to notice that the Authorised Version reverses the order of verse eight, compared to many manuscripts. The stronger evidence supports the reading given in most other translations: 'Remember Jesus Christ raised from among the dead, of the seed of David' (JND). It is easy to see how the change came to be introduced – it seems altogether more logical to follow the historical sequence in which incarnation ('of the seed of David') comes before the resurrection.[13] Given the weight of the manuscript evidence, however, the very fact that the critical reading is less obvious makes it more likely to be correct – it is far easier to imagine a scribe moving the reference to the seed of

---

[13] This is the order that Paul uses in Romans 1:3,4.

David before the mention of the resurrection than it is to imagine the reverse.

Accepting that 'Jesus Christ raised from among the dead, of the seed of David' is the correct order, we must ask ourselves why this is so. The answer to this question gets to the heart of the thrilling truth that Paul wishes Timothy to fill his mind with. When he suffers 'as a good soldier of Jesus Christ' (v. 3), he is suffering for the sake of One 'having been raised' from the dead. Paul's unusual use of the perfect participle here is noteworthy. It emphasises 'the lasting significance of Jesus' resurrection – that is, it is not just a historical event to be remembered but a truth holding promise for believers to be rehearsed over and over again'.[14] 'Raised' is a divine passive. It reminds us of the source of the power that accomplished the resurrection: God has done the raising.[15] The resurrection is a conquering, climactic, and incontestable demonstration of Divine power. No believer who keeps his mind on Jesus Christ having been raised from the dead can have any doubt about God's power to recompense his present sacrifice. It is proof positive that our 'labour is not in vain in the Lord' (1 Cor. 15:58), and a guarantee that suffering now will mean glory then.

Mighty though it undoubtedly is, resurrection is not the only assurance that the verse presents. The 'having been raised' One is the coming to reign One. This surely is the import of Paul's reference to the Seed of David.[16] It is not incarnation, in and of itself, that is in view, but rather the Messianic qualifications that Christ possesses as the Seed of David. The title reiterates the point made

---

[14] Towner, *Timothy*, 500.
[15] See the discussion in Mounce, *Pastoral Epistles*, 512.
[16] It is certainly not the case that the title 'is irrelevant in the context' (So Kelly, *Pastoral Epistles*, 177).

in the opening verses of chapter 1, for it reminds us that 'the gospel is rooted in history'.[17] But its chief purpose is to point us to the future, for it reminds us that He will reign – indeed, that 'He must reign' (1 Cor. 15:25). Its use here lays the foundation for the promise of verse 12 – 'if we suffer, we shall also reign with Him'. That promise has value because, and only because, He is risen and will reign.

This view of the verse accounts for another feature that some commentators have found puzzling: the order of the title 'Jesus Christ'. Christ Jesus is overwhelmingly the form that Paul prefers in the Pastoral Epistles – it occurs twenty-four times in the Pastorals, as compared to only six uses of 'Jesus Christ'.[18] In particular, this is the only time in 2 Timothy that this order occurs.[19] The explanation most often offered is it 'may suggest that it is borrowed from an early Christian creed of hymn already known by Timothy'.[20] That hypothesis, in the present state of knowledge, is impossible to prove and seems, in any case, unnecessary. The ordering reinforces the stress on the trajectory from suffering to glory: Jesus, the name of His humanity is followed by His messianic title. He has no future but glory, and (stupendous thought) His future is our future too.

It is worth stepping back for a moment from the detail of the passage to take in the broad significance of these Messianic references. In chapter 1 we looked to the past

---

[17] Paul M. Zehr, *1 & 2 Timothy, Titus*, Believers Church Bible Commentary, (Scottdale, PA: Herald Press, 2010), 178.

[18] 1 Tim. 6:3, 14; Tit. 1:1; 2:13; 3:6.

[19] Following the critical text. The KJV, by contrast, has 'Jesus Christ' in 1:10 and 2:3.

[20] Robert B. Wall, *1 & 2 Timothy and Titus*, The Two Horizons New Testament Commentary, (Grand Rapids, MI: Eerdmans, 2012), 242. See also Kelly, *Pastoral Epistles*, 177 and Towner, *Timothy*, 499n.4. Mounce *Pastoral Epistles* considers it 'doubtful that there is any significance to the order of the names' (511).

and learned that we have become part of something tremendously big. In chapter 2, we look to the future and learn the same lesson. If it is true that we have become part of a Divine programme that stretches backwards to the beginning of time, then it is also true that we have become part of a glorious and inexorable programme that culminates with Christ on the throne of the universe – and with us reigning with Him. Our present suffering makes sense because Christ has risen and will reign – and because we will reign with Him.

This remarkable truth is, Paul says, 'according to my gospel'. Paul's use of the possessive 'my' may anticipate the references later in the chapter to the false teachers who had deviated from the apostolic message, 'saying that the resurrection is past already' (v. 18). The thought here is not so much that this verse is a summary of the gospel. Rather, Paul is making the point that the template of the gospel is suffering followed by glory. That this should be true of Timothy – or of you and me – should be no surprise, for it was, in its fullest and deepest sense, true of 'Jesus Christ'.

Does it then make sense for the believer to endure, rather than evade, present suffering? Paul's answer is yes, for ours is a having-been-raised and soon-to-be-reigning Saviour, and the power that accomplished that for Christ will do the same for us.

Verse 9 Since verse 3 of this chapter, Paul has been dealing with the motivations that would encourage Timothy to heed his injunction to 'endure hardness, as a good soldier of Jesus Christ.' In verses 4 to 7, he outlined a rapid-fire succession of images, all hammering away at the same basic point – we should suffer and strive and sow now because of the recognition and reward and recompense that will follow in the future. The soldier, the athlete, and the farmer all demonstrate the priority of the future – they act in the present, because of the future. In verse 8, Paul began the sentence that is completed by this verse. It is a sentence that deals with the future and the power that guarantees it. By pointing us to Christ's resurrection and reign, Paul has reminded us that our future reward is underwritten, not just by God's promise, but by His power as well. Our resurrection is sure because Christ has risen, and our future reign is beyond doubt because of His Messianic prospects. And, the apostle reminds us this pattern – of present suffering and future glory – is 'according to my gospel'. This is the template that the gospel would lead us to expect. It is 'the way the Master went; should not the servant follow still?'[21]

And it is precisely this road of suffering that this particular servant is treading: 'for which I suffer hardship to the point of imprisonment as a criminal' (NET). In a few, economical words, Paul sketches in something of the extent of the suffering that he is enduring. But he begins by stressing the reason for it – it is for the gospel that he suffers hardship. Paul underscores this point, with some irony, in the words that he uses. The word 'gospel' means good news. For the sake of this good news, Paul 'suffers bad things' (*kakopatheō*) as a 'doer of bad things' (*kakourgos*). The word for suffering is closely related to that used in verse 3, linking the example of the apostle here with his exhortation earlier. Timothy had been called to be a co-sufferer, and now Paul is making sure that he understands what that might involve.

Paul's identification of his status as that of an 'evil doer' is also significant. The word translated thus is used

---

[21] Horatius Bonar, 'Go, labour on: spend and be spent', *Believers Hymn Book*, 387.

elsewhere in the Bible only in Luke 23 (vv. 32, 33, 39), where it describes the 'malefactors' who were crucified alongside the Lord Jesus. While the word can mean a 'simple good-for-nothing', in general it seems to have been reserved for the worse form of criminal and was used for violent criminals, murderers and, as in Luke, for those who were 'headed for crucifixion'.[22]

There is a tremendous pathos to the words, even at our remove. They must have seemed nearly heartbreaking to the tender Timothy, who had already shed tears over the apostle (1:4). Here was the great apostle, a man who had really been an 'evil doer' before he encountered Christ on the Damascus road. From that moment, his whole life had been consumed with the proclamation of the good news of the gospel, a message that is good and does good. He had poured himself out for the blessing of others. Now, as his life draws towards its close, he is incarcerated and forsaken, shackled not only with his chain but with the stigma and ignominy of being branded a criminal, a doer of bad things.

But the pathos is not the point. Paul is not writing these words as an exercise in self-pity, but to emphasise and exalt the power of God. In the darkness of the dungeon, imprisoned and bound, he picks up his pen and writes a defiant and glorious 'but'. 'I am bound', says Paul, 'but the word of God is not bound'. The Word of God is not bound. Before we look at the words in detail let the glorious truth of this sentence sweep over your soul. And let your enjoyment of these words be deepened by the certainty that they are true. This is not a vain cry of defiance. Paul is not shoring himself up against despair with empty words or false hope. The Word of God was not bound, nor has it been. Later in

---

[22] Ceslas Spicq, *Theological Lexicon of the New Testament* (trans. James D. Ernest), (Peabody, MA: Hendrickson, 1995), 2:241–243.

this epistle, he will give us an example of this: 'the Lord stood with me, and strengthened me; that by me the preaching might be fully known, and that all the Gentiles might hear' (4:17). Paul had preached to Nero – the Word of God was not bound. But we have already seen this truth in action at the beginning of this chapter – albeit in a far less dramatic way. Timothy was passing on the truth that he had received to faithful men. Those faithful men were teaching others also. The Word of God was not bound. Down through the ages, many of those faithful men – and faithful women too – would be bound. They would be bound, and beaten, and burned. Pontiffs and princes, sultans and socialists would do everything in their power to bind the messengers, but they could never bind the message. On and on it went, and on and on it goes, still unbound, still unlimited in all its majestic power. Luther put it well:

> *That word above all earthly powers—*
> *No thanks to them—abideth;*
> *The Spirit and the gifts are ours*
> *Through him who with us sideth.*
> *Let goods and kindred go,*
> *This mortal life also:*
> *The body they may kill:*
> *God's truth abideth still,*
> *His kingdom is for ever.*

The Word of God is not bound. The contrast between Paul's condition and the freedom of the message is heightened by the fact that the verb used here is a play on the word that Paul uses of his own bondage. It is 'an intensive present, emphasising the ongoing freedom of the gospel'.[23] It is important to ask what is meant by 'the

---

[23] Mounce, *Pastoral Epistles*, 514.

word of God' in this verse. Some commentators limit the expression to Paul's own preaching or to 'the proclamation of the gospel in dynamic terms'.[24] While these aspects are undoubtedly included, to limit its meaning too rigidly in this way seems undesirable. Rather, 'the expression "the word of God" points to the totality of God's verbal self-disclosure, whether verbal or written. The apostolic message did not exist, historically speaking, apart from the Old Testament writings that prepared the way for it and New Testament writings that quickly took shape as the gospel went forth. So while Paul may be speaking of God's saving message proclaimed, his understanding of "the word of God" should not be set at a distance from or in opposition to the canonical Scriptures.'[25]

From our perspective, the Word of God is essentially synonymous with the Scriptures. When the Scriptures are opened, the power of God is at work. A grasp of this truth has tremendous implications for all those who teach or preach. Whether we speak to sinners or to saints, we must realise that the power of our message does not lie in our own oratory or eloquence, but in the Word of God. In chapter 3, Paul will tell us about the comprehensive provision that is to be found in the Scriptures that ensure that the man of God is 'throughly furnished unto all good works' (3:17). Here he emphasises the power that is inherent in the Word of God that is not, and that cannot be bound. Why would we ever want to preach or to teach anything else?

Verse 10 Time and again in these verses, Paul has made the point that, for the believer, suffering now will mean glory then. Up to this point, the focus has been largely

---

[24] Towner, *Timothy*, 503.
[25] Yarbrough, *Letters to Timothy and Titus*, 378.

on the individual reward for faithful service. There has been a hint of a bigger picture in the last of the three pictures that Paul has called us to consider. The fact that the husbandman is first partaker of the coming crops hints that there are others who will share in the future blessings of his present toil. Now Paul develops this theme. He suffers 'all these things' not just in the expectation of future reward for himself, but in order to secure the future glory of others.

The force of the 'therefore' at the beginning of the verse makes it clear that there is a strong causal link between verses 8 and 9, and verse 10. In verses 8 and 9, Paul has called upon Timothy to remember that Christ has been raised and will reign. He has reminded Timothy, too, of the unconfinable power of the Word of God. We have seen already how the truth of these verses underwrites the lessons of verses 4–7. Now Paul tells us that it underlies his service – 'therefore' (that is, because verses 8 and 9 are true) he endures all things for the elect's sake. The word 'endure' is more general than Paul's earlier references to suffering. It carries the sense of 'remaining patiently under', and, coupled with 'all things' embraces every circumstance through which Paul is passing. Paul's confidence that he has a God Who has the power to raise Christ and a programme to see Him reign allows him patiently to endure with the blessing of the elect in view.

By way of clearing the ground, it should be explicitly said that there is no thought here of Paul's sufferings having, in and of themselves, any salvific or meritorious value for the elect. He suffers with their blessing in view, but the sufferings themselves convey no blessing upon them.

Not a few commentators have understood this verse to say that Paul endures all things so that the elect might get saved. This view 'requires an unlikely use of the term "elect", which in the Old and New Testaments refers to the people of God, and reflects an overly narrow view of the concept of salvation'.[26] Moreover, it fails to do justice to the context of the verses or to the language used. Here, as elsewhere, Paul is using the term 'the elect' to describe those who are already saved. The term emphasises the privileged standing of those who are saved.[27] It stresses the value of the apostle's labour on their behalf and explains why their blessing is such a powerful motivation. Paul is enduring all things for the sake of those who are special to God, and that gives his suffering no ordinary significance.

The goal of Paul's endurance, then, is not so much that sinners are brought to saving faith, but that the elect 'may also obtain the salvation which is in Christ Jesus with eternal glory'. Paul does not want these believers, who are so incalculably precious to God, just to limp across the threshold of glory with empty hands and an uncrowned head, 'saved; yet so as by fire' (1 Cor. 3:15). Rather, he desires for these believers what Peter calls an abundant entrance 'into the everlasting kingdom of our Lord and Saviour Jesus Christ' (2 Pet. 1:11). His goal is that 'they may also obtain

---

[26] Towner, *Timothy and Titus*, 504. Towner's point deserves emphasis – the term elect is never used in the NT of the unsaved, and things are said of the elect that are only true of those who are saved. For example, Romans 8:33 tells us that no charge can be brought against God's elect and Titus 1:1 tells us that 'God's elect' have faith (whether we understand that faith to be objective or subjective makes no difference to this argument). See, for a more detailed discussion Mark Sweetnam, 'Truth in the Pastoral Epistles (5)', *Truth & Tidings*, (Dec, 2017), 68:12, http://truthandtidings.com/2017/12/truth-in-the-pastoral-epistles-5-its-revelation-3/.

[27] Witherington makes the interesting suggestion that this 'could be a reference to salvation for Paul's fellow Jews'. This would not be altogether incongruous in the context, but there is hardly sufficient evidence in the passage to make it more than speculative. Ben Witherington III, *Letters and Homilies for Hellenized Christians (Vol. 1)*, (Nottingham: Apollos, 2006), 332.

salvation ... with eternal glory'. 'Also' gives us a lovely insight into the heart of the apostle. He was no maverick, seeking only his own glory. He knew that he would obtain the salvation with eternal glory. He was confident that 'a crown of righteousness' (4:8) was laid up for him. But he longed for others to share the glory and the crown.

A number of things confirm that this is the correct interpretation of this verse. Firstly, we should notice the word translated 'obtain' (*tygchanō*). This has at its root the idea of hitting the mark and, in this context, means 'to reach, attain, obtain, get'.[28] The word, in this form, occurs on only one other occasion in the New Testament, in Hebrews 11:35: 'others were tortured, not accepting deliverance; that they might *obtain* a better resurrection'. There, as here, the emphasis lies on the future and the eschatological. There, as here, we are looking forward, not back.

Secondly, this interpretation gives due weight to the expression 'with eternal glory'. The context of this passage, with its emphasis on reward, makes it clear that Paul is not just thinking of the fact that every believer will be glorified. 'Whilst all who are saved will be glorified, the next verse [along with those that have gone before] shows that the apostle is thinking of the special rewards to be given to those who are faithful to Christ'.[29] The use of 'the same expression in 1 Peter 5:10 in a similar context supports this view.'[30]

This verse, then, continues the chapter's focus on the future. It tells us that, because of his confidence in God and in the unstoppable power of His Word, Paul is

---

[28] Thayer, *s.v.*
[29] W.E. Vine, *The Collected Writings of W.E. Vine (Vol. 3)*, (Nashville, TN: Thomas Nelson, 1996), 213.
[30] J.R. Baker, *What the Bible Teaches: II Timothy*, (Kilmarnock: John Ritchie Ltd, 1983), 345.

willing patiently to endure everything that comes his way, so that he might help God's elect arrive at their future salvation with a full load of eternal glory.

The truth of this verse has some searching practical implications for us. We can learn much from Paul's attitude to his fellow believers. Paul may have lived in competition with himself (1 Cor. 9:26, 27), but he never viewed other believers with a competitive spirit. He sought to bless and build them up, never to damage and drag them down. His commitment to their best interests went well beyond words – he appreciated their value to God and was happy to 'spend and be spent' (2 Cor. 12:15) on their behalf. Would that we desired the blessing and progress of others as ardently as we desire our own.

The verse also underlines for us the importance of Scripture. We form part of God's elect, and Paul had our wellbeing in view, just as much as that of believers in the first century. The goal of his service was our eternal glory. Today, we are the beneficiaries of that service largely through the epistles that he wrote. They have a crucial role in ensuring our eternal glory. If you doubt this, just imagine trying to live a Christian life without having access to any of Paul's epistles. How would you understand the gospel, the believer's relationship to the law, or how a local church should operate and be ordered? So much of what we know about living for and faithfully serving God, we know because of the patient endurance of the Apostle Paul. If we want eternal reward – and surely we all do – then we cannot ignore the fruits of his service to God and for us. To disregard, disparage, or disown his contribution to Scripture is an insult to his service and an impediment to our own reward.

vv. 11–13   Suffering and the Future

2 Timothy 2:11–13 bring this section of the epistle, with its focus on present suffering and future reward, to its conclusion. It does so by means of a 'faithful saying', the last, in terms of time, of five occasions when this expression occurs in the Pastoral Epistles (1 Tim. 1:15, 3:1, 4:9; 2 Tim. 2:11, Tit. 3:8). The significance of this expression has been the subject of much debate. There is a lack of consensus on whether the faithful sayings precede or follow the statement: 'five times in PE the phrase ... rings out like a fanfare of trumpets, as if to direct the attention of the reader to some significant truth, and yet, despite this evident intention on the part of the author, scholars ancient and modern have been uncertain where they are supposed to be looking.'[31] Similarly, there has been much discussion about the function of the expression – is it intended to affirm the truthfulness of what is said, or does it (also) indicate that Paul is quoting from pre-existing material from another source? Whether or not Paul is marking the inclusion of material from another source is, and is likely to remain, in the sphere of speculation. It seems much more certain that he uses the expression to emphasise material 'that Timothy or Titus can and should take with utmost seriousness, to the point of appropriating personally and completely'.[32] Beyond that, the use of the term 'faithful' serves a polemical purpose, whereby Paul 'in one motion, rearticulates his gospel (and corresponding aspects of teaching), asserts its authenticity and apostolic authority, and alienates the opposing teaching that, by implication ... does not belong to the category

---

[31] R. Alastair Campbell, 'Identifying the Faithful Sayings in the Pastoral Epistles', *Journal for the Study of the New Testament*, 54 (1994), 73–86, 73.
[32] Yarbrough, *Letters to Timothy and Titus*, 64.

denoted by the term [faithful]'.[33] This is the point that we must not lose sight of in the detail of the discussion. Paul is emphatically articulating vital truth and he wants Timothy – and us – to sit up and take notice. These are weighty words, demanding our careful consideration.

The 'faithful saying' found in verses 11–13 'is as complex as it is compressed'.[34] These verses show signs of careful, even poetic, structuring, which has led some commentators to suggest that they represent part of a hymn.[35] It is certainly the case that they share with other putative New Testament hymn quotations the trait of doctrinal richness – a characteristic that we should still seek in our own hymnody.[36] However, the lines have 'all the marks of having been shaped by Paul for insertion here.'[37] The use of the '*syn*' prefix in the verb 'die with' picks up on its use with the verb 'to suffer' in 2:3, and both the vocabulary and the thought of the lines mean that they feel wholly of a piece with both the argument of this section and the atmosphere of the epistle as a whole.

The saying is composed of four conditional ('if … then') sentences, followed by an explanatory note. The lines group in couplets – the first two are positive, the second two negative. The first half of each statement deals with the character of our Christian service in the present, the second with the future and eternal implications of our present and temporal actions. The

---

[33] Towner, *Timothy*, 144, 5.
[34] Wall, *1 & 2 Timothy and Titus*, 246.
[35] See, for example, Fee, *1 & 2 Timothy*, 248, Mounce, *Pastoral Epistles*, 515 and Stott, *2 Timothy*, 63.
[36] See the discussion in Mark Sweetnam, *Worship: The Christian's Highest Calling*, (Lisburn: Scripture Teaching Library, 2013), 101–3.
[37] Towner, *Timothy*, 507.

presentation gives the material a 'rhetorical impact and gravity' that survives even in translation.[38]

Verses 11–13 act as a bridge between the two sections of this chapter. The 'of these things' with which Paul commences verse 14 clearly indicates that these verses are closely connected with the argument that follows. However, we should not miss the fact that the faithful saying begins with the word 'for'. This serves to link the words back beyond the introductory formula to the content of verse 10, and to anchor these verses firmly in the context of the opening section of the chapter. More immediately, the linking 'for' indicates that verses 11b–13 expand on Paul's motivation as outlined in verse 10. This link emphasises what we have already seen – that when Paul speaks about 'obtaining the salvation which is in Christ Jesus with eternal glory' he is thinking about salvation in its future and eschatological aspect.

Verse 11 The first statement – 'if we be dead with Him' – is, perhaps, the most difficult portion of these lines to interpret. What does it mean to 'be dead' with Christ?[39] Some commentators attempt to answer this question by referring to Romans 6:8: 'Now if we be dead with Christ, we believe that we shall also live with Him'. That passage uses the same verb and tense as this verse to describe the believer's judicial death to sin through union with Christ. Although Romans 6:8 is not speaking about conversion, *per se*, a number of commentators have, on the basis of this link, understood dying with Christ in 2 Timothy 2:11 to refer to conversion.[40] It is an appealing

---

[38] Towner, *Timothy*, 508.
[39] The verb is in the aorist and can be rendered 'have died with' (JND, ESV) or 'died with' (RV, NET).
[40] So Towner, *Timothy*, 509, and Yarbrough, *Letters to Timothy and Titus*, 380; and Witherington III, *Letters*, 332. Cf Kelly, *Exposition*, 220–221, who sees a reference to Romans 6:8, but who does not conflate this with conversion.

consequence of this that the first couplet then moves from the past to the present, from conversion to the ongoing endurance of the Christian life. There are, however, a number of difficulties with this view. Conflating the believer's death with Christ and conversion fails to do justice to the teaching of Romans 6. Moreover, it is difficult to account for the relevance of conversion to the argument that Paul has been making in the chapter so far. The clear thrust of the section that is now drawing to a close has been that suffering for the gospel now makes sense in light of future reward. It is not clear what a return to the moment of conversion contributes to this line of thought.

This view that the expression 'died with Christ' points us back to conversion is not universal. There is a (justly) minority view that sees in the expression a reference to baptism.[41] John Stott, by contrast, argues that 'the death with Christ which is here mentioned must refer, according to the context, not to our death to *sin* through union with Christ in His death, but rather to our death to *self* and to *safety*, as we take up the cross and follow Christ.'[42] 'That this is the meaning' he argues 'seems plain from the fact that to 'have died with Christ' and 'to endure' are parallel expressions.' While it is true that the statements are parallel, it is not clear that they are parallel in the way that he suggests, and the parallelism that does exist neither compels his explanation nor makes it obviously correct.

Another, more viable, alternative is that the expression refers to physical death with Christ – that is, to martyrdom. Such a reference would be 'especially

---

[41] See Mounce, *Pastoral Epistles*, 516 and Wall, *Timothy*, 246.
[42] Stott, *2 Timothy*, 63, emphasis in original. Kelly, *Pastoral Epistles*, 179–180 combines these views: 'This dying with Christ ... [is] the death to sin and self which every Christian undergoes in baptism.'

[fitting] in a letter which is looking at Paul's own death'[43] and is clearly relevant to the emphasis on present suffering and future reward that runs through this section. The use of the aorist tense for 'died with' does not necessarily mitigate against this view. The tense used allows the expression to be rendered 'if we shall have,' or, 'If at any time we have'.[44] Rather than pointing to the past, the use of the aorist may emphasise the nature of martyrdom as a 'single definitive act of self-devotion'.[45] Mounce argues that this 'is an unusual choice of words to express martyrdom', but that argument hardly seems sustainable in light of the fact that in Mark 14:31, one of only two other occasions in the New Testament where this word is used, it refers to precisely that.

As Hendriksen points out, this view of the passage need not mean 'that believers (including Paul and Timothy) are pictured as having at any time already experienced the martyr's death but rather as being fully resigned to it and to all the afflictions which precede it.'[46] Nor should this be understood as making resurrection life dependent upon martyrdom – rather the point is that even if our present suffering reaches its climax in martyrdom, resurrection and eternal life with Christ must certainly follow.[47] While it would evidently be unwise to be dogmatic, given the range of opinion

---

[43] Marshall, *Pastoral Epistles*, 739.
[44] W. Hendriksen, *I–II Timothy and Titus*, New Testament Commentary, (Grand Rapids, MI: Baker, 1957), 256.
[45] J.H. Bernard, *The Pastoral Epistles*, (Cambridge: Cambridge University Press, 1906), 121.
[46] Hendriksen, *Timothy*, 257.
[47] This addresses Witherington's objection to the martyrdom view on the basis that 'the 'we' makes this a remark about all Christians' (Witherington, *Letters*, 332).

outlined above, martyrdom seems to be the view that best fits with the context of the passage.[48]

Among the advantages of this martyrdom view is the fact that it makes it clear that living with Christ refers to resurrection. The wider context of the passage and the thought flow of these verses both make a reference to anything other than future resurrection life a highly improbable reading. These verses link two references to the importance of resurrection. In verse 8, Paul has called on Timothy to 'remember … Jesus Christ … raised from the dead according to my gospel'. In verses 17 and 18, he warns Timothy about the corrosive effects of the false teaching 'that the resurrection is past already'. To see living with Christ as anything other than resurrection, then, not only disregards the insistent focus on the future that has marked the whole section from verse 1 to 10, but also ignores the explicit emphasis on resurrection in the immediate context.

To see living with Christ as something present also destroys the structure and symmetry of these lines. Each of the four statements deals with a present 'if' and a future 'then', echoing in miniature the argument of this whole section. In addition, the structure of these lines means that there is a clear synthetic parallelism between the living of verse 11 and the reigning of verse 12. The expressions 'do not express an identical thought, but there is progressive correspondence between the two propositions'.[49] To see living as something present and reigning as future destroys this parallelism.

It seems clear, then, that living with Christ, in this verse, is speaking about future, eschatological,

---

[48] Perhaps there is something to be said for the view espoused by Fee, 1 & 2 Timothy, 249–50, who sees conversion, baptism, and martyrdom co-existing in the passage.

[49] Hendriksen, Timothy and Titus, 256.

resurrection life. Although this conclusion seems obvious, it poses problems for those commentators who read 'having died' through the lens of Romans 6:8. Consistency requires them, perforce, to read 'living with Him' through the same lens, and to argue that 'living with Christ' refers to the present life of the believer. The forced and unconvincing nature of this reading and the violence that it does to the structure of these verses and their relationship to their context are the clearest demonstrations that there is something amiss with this understanding of the passage.[50]

All of this close-grained and rather nit-picking analysis is necessary for our understanding of this verse. But we ought not, amongst the thickets of the debate, to lose sight of the vital, daunting, and glorious point that Paul is making in this opening statement of the faithful saying. Even though we may not be called upon to be faithful unto death, faithfulness unto death is the standard for our Christian service. It was to that standard that Paul called Timothy. And he made that call in the full knowledge that his death was imminent. At a spot on the *Via Ostiensis*, just a short time after he wrote these words, Paul did die with Christ. From a human perspective, it hardly seems a fitting end for a man who was an apostle 'according to the promise of life which is in Christ Jesus' (1:1). But that human perspective misses the point altogether. Paul's executors might rob him of the possession of life with the stroke of a sword, but they could never rob him of the promise of life, nor could they ever prize asunder the cause and the

---

[50] This is especially true of commentators who take the baptism view, for example, Mounce, *Pastoral Epistles*, 516 and Wall, *Timothy*, 246. Towner, *Timothy*, 509 allows for both, but acknowledges that 'the eschatological aspect of this promise is probably uppermost in mind'.

consequence that faithful saying welded together: 'If we be dead with Him, we shall also live with Him'.

Verse 12 With a sense of regret that the verse divisions in this section so poorly follow the flow of Paul's argument, we come to the second positive statement: 'If we endure, we will also reign with him' (ESV, NET). As with the previous statement, the language used anchors this statement firmly to its context. The word 'endure' (translated 'suffer' in the AV) is the same as that used of Paul in verse 10, linking this promise with the example of the apostle.[51] Similarly, the thought of reigning with Christ echoes the messianic future implicitly evoked by Paul's reference to 'Jesus Christ of the seed of David' (v. 8).

To endure is to persevere – to put one's head down into the wind of adversity and keep on moving forward. It includes, too, the idea of 'holding one's ground patiently in trouble or affliction'.[52] It is neither a glamorous nor a glorious concept, but it is linked here with a glorious promise – 'we shall ... reign with Him'. 'If', of course, does sound a note of warning, for it reminds us of the possibility that we might not endure. However, the emphasis is more upon the promise – if we endure, as we can and as we should, then the certain outcome is this: we shall reign with Him. The truth that the believer's present service and suffering will be recompensed in a future reign with Christ is expressed on a number of occasions throughout the New Testament.[53] The idea that Christ's coming kingdom is somehow irrelevant or peripheral to the believers of this dispensation is difficult to substantiate from Scripture. The Millennium is not something that we will

---

[51] Paul uses this word elsewhere only in Rom. 12:12 and 1 Cor. 13:7.
[52] Fee, *1 & 2 Timothy*, 250.
[53] See, for example, Acts 14:22 and 2 Thess. 1:4,5.

experience as detached spectators, but as active participants. The role that we will play then is determined by the faithfulness of our service now.[54] The promise is not that if we are successful, or popular, or acclaimed we will reign with Him. The question will be – did I endure?

It seems to have been William MacDonald who adapted lines originally penned by Frank Sweet to memorably express a challenging truth:

> *A noble life is not a blaze*
> *Of sudden glory won,*
> *But just an adding up of days*
> *In which God's will is done.*[55]

The reminder is salutary. But, on the basis of this passage, let us grasp the truth that an enduring and faithful 'adding up of days' will issue, ultimately, in a 'blaze of glory won' for if we endure we will reign with Him.

At this point, the 'faithful saying' changes direction. Heretofore the emphasis has been on rewards for faithfulness. While it is true that the repeated 'if' implicitly allows for the possibility that faithfulness would not be the course chosen, the focus has been on the rewards that faithfulness gives, and the assumption has been that Timothy will heed the opening exhortation to endure hardship. Now, however, as the section draws to a close, a note of warning is sounded. Timothy had a real choice to make. So do we. And while Paul's confidence in Timothy suggests that the outcome

---

[54] Kelly's response to the idea 'that the saints reign now' is worth noting. '[It] is unequivocal error. It is wrong morally as well as dogmatically. We shall reign with Christ; but even He sits on His Father's throne as yet. He waits to receive His own throne; and so do we much more' (Kelly, *Exposition*, 221).

[55] William MacDonald, *One Day at a Time: Truths to Live By* (Everyday Publications, 1985), entry for January 10.

of his choice was never really in question, we are not all Timothy, and we do well to consider the warnings, as well as the promises of the section.

A useful place to start is to notice that the warning sounded is for believers: 'if we deny Him, He also will deny us'. The use of 'we' here, as well as in the first two statements, making it unlikely that these warnings are addressed to a different audience than the opening promises. Appreciating this will help us to understand exactly how we are to understand the force of the word 'deny' or 'disown'. This word is used elsewhere in the New Testament of Peter's denial of Christ (e.g., Mt. 26:70, Mk 14:68, Lk. 22:57, Jn 18:25) It is also used to describe Israel's response to Moses ('This Moses whom they refused' Acts 7:35) and to Christ (Acts 3:13, 14). Peter uses the word of those apostates who deny 'the Lord that bought them' (2 Pet. 2:1), and the Lord Jesus used it in Matthew 10:33: 'whosoever shall deny Me before men, him will I also deny before My Father which is in heaven.' In the Pastoral Epistles, Paul uses the word of denying the faith (1 Tim. 5:8), denying the power of godliness (2 Tim. 3:5), denying God (Tit. 1:16) and, positively, of 'denying ungodliness and worldly lusts' (Tit. 2:12). Though the basic meaning of the word is the same in each of these instances, and while it always speaks of something serious, it is evident that there is a significant difference of degree between the way in which Peter denied the Lord, for instance, and the way in which the apostates of which he later wrote do.

The embracive nature of this warning, along with the context of the verse suggests that we are not dealing here with apostasy, but with something closer to Peter's actions at the high priest's fire. In the context of this section of the epistle, disowning Christ is the inverse of choosing to 'endure hardship' (2:3). It is the course chosen by 'all they which are in Asia' and by Phygellus and Hermogenes (1:15). It appears to be this sort of denial, rather that than doctrinal departure exemplified by Hymenaeus and Philetus (2:17), that is in view here.

That this is the correct understanding of the expression in this context is confirmed by the fact that the second disowning (by Christ is implicit, though not stated) is opposed to reigning with Christ. Those who deny Christ, who disown him in order to evade shame and suffering, will not please their commander (v. 4) win the crown (v. 5), or reap the fruit (v. 6). The recognition and reward that would have followed faithfulness to Christ will be denied them. None of this is to suggest that it is not the case that those who deny Christ in apostasy will be denied eternally by Him. But that is not the focus of Paul's argument in this passage. Nor should this make us regard this as a less solemn statement. To choose a path free from suffering by denying Christ might seem like the easy option, but it will have eternal and costly consequences.

Verse 13 'if we are faithless, he remains faithful' (*ESV*). 'Faithless' (*apisteō*) could be translated 'unbelieving' and that is the sense in which the word is used in every other New Testament occurrence. However, the fact that the positive form of the same word (*pistos*) is used in the second clause makes it clear that 'faithless' or 'unfaithful' (*NET*) is the preferable rendering. Otherwise, Paul would be saying 'if we believe not; yet He believes', and the improbability of that translation is obvious.

What is less clear is the character and extent of this faithlessness. It is likely that the primary concern here is on faithfulness to Christ, rather than adherence to doctrinal orthodoxy, especially as the focus in the second part of the verse is on His person. However, it would be artificial and unhelpful to distinguish sharply between faithfulness to Christ and adherence to the truth. Moreover, the shift to doctrinal issues in the following verses suggests that faithfulness here is to be understood in a fairly comprehensive sense.

As with the 'disowning' of verse 12, there is scope for some debate about the extent of the faithlessness that is referred to in this verse. While it could describe the action of the apostate, here, as in verse 12, Paul's use of the pronoun 'we' suggests that this faithlessness could, potentially, characterise believers. Structurally, the verb parallels 'endure' and the fact that both are in the present tense suggests that this faithlessness is the inverse of enduring. It may refer to something less decisive than 'disowning', an ongoing accumulation of small disloyalties to Christ. Such moments of disloyalty are likely less rare in our lives than any of us would care to admit. It may not be that we disown Christ with the directness that Peter did, but faced with a choice between standing up and laying low, between enduring and yielding, how often do we choose the apparently easier option of faithlessness to the immediately costly but ultimately rewarding alternative of suffering hardship?

The structure of these lines up to this point means that, from a purely literary point of view, we would expect this fourth statement to end with 'He is faithless'. From a theological point of view, however, such a conclusion would be altogether untenable, and Paul concludes the faithful word with a positive affirmation: 'He abideth faithful'.

Commentators are divided as to whether this should be understood as a reassuring promise or as a solemn warning. If we understand 'faithless' to refer to apostasy, then clearly the second alternative is the only tenable one, and the faithfulness in view must be Divine faithfulness in judging those apostates. This view also prevails amongst some of those who do not necessarily understand faithlessness as apostasy.[56] While it is undoubtedly the case that Christ's inability to deny Who He is means 'carrying out his threats … as well as His promises', it is not clear that this is what these words are intended to convey.[57]

The other view is that these words are to be understood as a reassuring promise for the believer. On this view, Christ's faithfulness is introduced to remind Timothy that, while his faithfulness is profoundly important, ultimately his salvation is not guaranteed by his faithfulness to God, but by God's faithfulness to him.[58] Apart from the fact that this interpretation better fits the context of these verses, there are a number of reasons to support this interpretation. In the New Testament, Divine faithfulness almost invariably has God's people as its object, and the implications of that faithfulness are always blessing for those who belong to Him.[59] Given how consistent this emphasis is throughout the New Testament, it is unlikely that this verse is speaking about Christ's faithfulness to Himself,

---

[56] John Stott, 2 Timothy, (Nottingham: Inter-Varsity Press, 1999), 64; Vine, Collected Writings (Vol. 3), 214; and Yarbrough, Letters to Timothy and Titus, 382.

[57] Hendriksen, I–II Timothy and Titus, 260.

[58] So Fee, 1 & 2 Timothy, 249–51 and Mounce, Pastoral Epistles, 517, 8. Towner, Timothy, 514 agrees that this may be the meaning but offers the alternative suggestion that the verse provides reassurance that 'whatever befalls the church, Christ will remain faithful to it.'

[59] See 1 Cor. 1:9, 10:13; 1 Thess. 5:24; 2 Thess. 3:3; Heb. 2:17, 10:23, 11:11; 1 Pet. 4:19; 1 Jn 1:9; Rev. 1:5; 3:14, 19:11. Heb. 3:2 is perhaps the only occasion where the emphasis is faithfulness to God. While it is true that Rev. 3:14–21 does warn of judgement, it also promises blessing. That Scripture speaks of God's faithfulness in this way is a remarkable fact and worthy of much greater consideration than is possible here.

or that its emphasis is on judgement. It is altogether more in keeping with New Testament usage to see here a promise of Christ's faithfulness to His own, even if they fail in their faithfulness to Him. It is moreover, significant that the verse does not say that Christ is faithful, but that He continues, or remains, faithful. This is most easily accounted for as a reassurance that no change or failure on the part of the believer can bring about an alteration or diminution in the faithfulness of Christ.

Christ's faithfulness is grounded in His character for 'He cannot deny Himself'. The NLT rendering nicely catches the sense of the expression: 'for He cannot deny Who He is'. Christ will always act in perfect consistency with His own character: 'the ground or proof of His abiding fidelity lies in the blessed fact of His unchanging truth.'[60]

So it is that this section, which has dealt in the most solemn and searching way with the importance of faithful, unremitting service even in the face of opposition and suffering closes with a reminder that our salvation is not, in the final analysis, dependent upon us – it is not performance based. That reminder is grounds for comfort, but not complacency, because, though our salvation is not performance based, our reward most assuredly is. There is a 'well done' to be achieved, a trophy to be won, and a harvest to be reaped. There is 'eternal glory' to be gained and a reign to be enjoyed. But they are only available to those who 'endure hardness, as a good soldier of Jesus Christ' (2:3). May God grant us grace to be found among their number.

---

[60] Kelly, *Exposition*, 222.

2:14–26 THE ACTIVITIES OF THE MAN OF GOD

vv. 14, 15   Studying

Verse 14 begins a new section of the epistle – the focus shifts from Timothy's anticipation and its implications for his present service, to his activity as a man of God. The imperatives of this section are arranged in two groups of three (vv. 14–16, 24–26), each following the pattern negative, positive, negative. The first triad focuses primarily on doctrine, the second on personal behaviour. Between the two series of imperatives comes a pair of architectural metaphors, which stress the need for holiness – for freedom from both doctrinal and moral defilement. The focus on motivation, a pronounced feature of verses 1–13 of the chapter, continues here, but in these verses the motivation is less eschatological reward (though that never entirely recedes from view) than the benefit and blessing of others. There is a particular stress in these verses on the consequences of teaching. This makes them solemn reading for anyone who has the responsibility to teach God's people, and they have valuable lessons for us all about the power of speech to help or to hinder our fellow believers. Our speech matters more than we sometimes seem to think.

Verse 14 provides the transition between the two sections of this chapter – 'these things' points us back to the verses that have gone before – particularly vv. 8–13. Timothy was to remember that truth for himself (v. 8) and he was to remind the believers of it too.[61] It is unsafe for teachers or those taught to lose sight of the fundamental truths outlined in the preceding verses – there is always a place for a ministry of 'putting in mind'.

---

[61] In the Greek, there is no object for the verb 'remind', but it seems obvious that Paul has the believers among whom Timothy laboured in view.

Paul exhorts Titus to the same activity (Tit. 3:1), and Peter identified a similar emphasis in his ministry (2 Pet. 1:12). These Scriptures provide no mandate for the mechanical repetition of teaching and no excuse for the unprepared and unexercised teacher. But they do free the teacher of Scripture from the pursuit of novelty, from the pressure to say something that has never been said before. There is tremendous merit in reminding the saints about the fundamentals of the Christian faith.

That Paul is not thinking about teaching that is purely mechanical or merely rote is emphasised by the verb he uses as he turns to the negative aspect of Timothy's teaching: 'charge' (a present imperative) is a word that calls for earnest, forceful, and solemn speech. Paul charges Timothy twice in these epistles (1 Tim. 5:21, 2 Tim. 4:1) and the force and solemnity of his words on those occasions is to be matched by Timothy's own teaching. Timothy had, as all teachers of Scripture should, first felt for himself the weight of the ministry that he communicated to others.

The charge in this instance was a very specific one – Timothy was to urge the believers not to 'strive about words'. This phrase translates the Greek word, *logomacheō*, which is found only here in the New Testament and which literally means 'battling over words'. The expression does not have in view a careful attention to the words of Scripture or the detailed and painstaking effort to understand exactly what those words convey. Nor does it proscribe careful and courteous discussion or debate over the fine details of exegesis. Rather, it refers to a quarrelsome pedantry that finds in the text of Scripture fuel for arid and unedifying dispute. Although such an attitude is unlikely to indicate that the person that holds it is in good spiritual condition, Paul is less interested in the diagnosis of their pathology, than the impact that this quarrelling will have upon others. Firstly, such disputing will be 'to no profit'. That is, it serves no useful purpose, it is a waste of time. But its dangers do not stop there, for it also has the potential to 'subvert' the hearers. 'Subvert' translates '*katastrophē*', the word from which we get our English word catastrophe. It means 'overthrow' or 'demolish'. Paul is concerned here, not with the minor discouragement of the hearers or with some readily remedied blip in their spiritual progress, but with spiritual catastrophe that could shake these believers to their core and permanently and irreparably damage their usefulness for God.

This a sobering verse for anyone who endeavours to teach the Word of God. It brings before us very clearly the need to be mindful of the consequences of our teaching. Our motive in teaching should be the benefit of the saints. It is alarming to contemplate the possibility that our teaching – in ministry, Bible reading contributions, or whatever form it might take – should be without profit, merely useless. How much worse, for us, as well as for our hearers, if our teaching should mean spiritual catastrophe for our audience. The blessing of believers must be the motive of our teaching – if we are aiming at anything less, we had far better not teach at all.

Verse 15 Timothy had, as we have, a responsibility to his hearers. Above that, though, he had, as we have, a responsibility to God, and it is this responsibility that is introduced in verse 15. This verse has often been treated as a manifesto for Bible study – and it is, even though the translation of the opening word in the *AV* may give it a somewhat different emphasis than what Paul intended. Up to the nineteenth century, 'study' could be used to mean 'to strive towards, set one's mind on, devote oneself to' (OED), a sense that it has now lost, but which accurately captures the meaning of the Greek word, which can also be rendered 'make every effort' (NET), 'be diligent' (HCSB), or, less satisfactorily, in terms of English style, at least, 'do your best' (NIV, ESV). Paul is calling Timothy to exert himself with a view to presenting himself 'approved of God' and 'an unashamed workman'.[62]

The word 'shew' or 'present' can be used of the presentation of an offering, but here (as in 2 Cor. 4:14, 11:2, Eph. 5:27, Col. 1:22, 28) it has rather the sense of presenting to a judge for inspection. 'Approved unto God' includes something more than just winning Divine approbation. The word has the idea of approved by testing (it is translated 'tried' in James 1:12), and was used of metals and coins. So, while Timothy was to preach with the blessing of his hearers in view, what he taught was to meet the test of Divine appraisal. This fact removes any idea of the subjective or the situational from the idea of aiming for the blessing of our hearers – what we teach will only be of blessing to man if it is approved of God and in accordance with His Word.

The reality of Divine scrutiny is reiterated in the image of the 'workman that needeth not to be ashamed'. To encourage Timothy to be an 'unashamed worker' is, implicitly, to raise the dreadful possibility of being a worker who does need to be ashamed by the poor standard of his workmanship. The image of the workman, or labourer, also reminds us that diligent effort is demanded – 'rightly dividing the word of truth' is the work of a worker, not the diversion of the dilettante.

But what, precisely, is involved in 'rightly dividing the word of truth'. Since the days of C.I. Scofield, at least, the phrase has been used to refer to the dispensational

---

[62] Towner, *Timothy*, 520.

interpretation of Scripture. 'Rightly dividing the word of truth' certainly includes properly distinguishing the dispensations, but it would be to limit the meaning of the expression to only one aspect – however important – of the correct interpretation of Scripture. 'Rightly dividing', which occurs only here in the New Testament, is a difficult phrase to interpret, but it involves the idea of ploughing a straight furrow, laying a straight road, or cutting a straight line. Whatever the precise shade of metaphor Paul intended – and the idea of cutting certainly resonates with the architectural language used in verses 19, 20 – the sense is clearly that of correct interpretation, in contrast to Hymenaeus and Philetus who 'concerning the truth have erred' – swerved, or missed the mark. Timothy is to carefully and accurately handle the 'word of truth', cutting a straight and undeviating line. Some commentators have limited 'rightly dividing' to teaching, but, as the counter-example of Hymenaeus and Philetus demonstrates, that is to make an artificial and unwarranted distinction between exegesis and exposition. Their erroneous understanding of Scripture was expressed in their gangrenous teaching: Timothy's correct understanding, his 'right division' of the 'word of truth', obtained by dint of diligent and careful labour, would be expressed in his own teaching.

In this discussion, we have treated 'the word of truth' as though it were synonymous with Scripture. This is neither accidental nor incidental. There is little reason to question that the 'word [*logos*] of truth' is effectively a reference to the Scriptures. While it is true that *logos* has a connotation of utterance, it is used in the New Testament to refer either to a specific Scripture (e.g., Jn 10:35 and Rom. 9:6), or to the Old Testament or Scripture as a whole (e.g., Mk 7:9–13 and Heb. 4:12). In Ephesians

1:13 'the word of truth' is defined as 'the gospel of your salvation' but there is no reason to confine this expression to the message that we might preach to the unconverted. For Paul, 'the gospel' was conterminous with 'the faith' and 'the truth' (note v. 18), and for us, those expressions are conterminous with the Bible.[63] May we seek to rightly divide it, so that we may be unashamed workers, approved unto God.

vv. 16–19   Shunning

Verse 16 provides the third doctrinal imperative of this section of the epistle. Timothy was to charge others to avoid quarrelling about words (v. 14) and was himself to cut a straight line through the Word of God, conscious that his handling of Scripture would be subject to Divine appraisal (v. 15). Now he is instructed about his own reaction to valueless teaching, described here as 'profane and vain babblings'. 'Profane' means unhallowed or godless, and 'vain babblings' are empty and meaningless talk – a meaning that is excellently and onomatopoetically communicated by the KJV translation.[64] Timothy is to have nothing to do with this irreverent chatter – he is to 'shun' it – literally to turn his back upon it. And he is to shun it because of the inevitable consequences for such discourse – those who engage in it will make progress ('increase') in altogether the wrong direction – 'unto more ungodliness'. 'More' reinforces the idea of progress, emphasising that these individuals are already on a godless trajectory. Their empty babbling has no power to arrest or reverse their decline only to accelerate their decline. In contrast to the straight way that Timothy is to forge, those who indulge

---

[63] See Yarbrough, *Letters to Timothy and Titus*, 378, 386, 519.
[64] The word occurs elsewhere in the NT only in 1 Tim. 6:20 – the argument here closely parallels that section.

in profane babbling are on a downward spiral – moving forwards, certainly, but making progress only in ungodliness.

Verses 17, 18 The fact that false teaching leads to increasing ungodliness is particularly resonant in the Pastoral Epistles, where there is a repeated emphasis on godliness of life as the product of sound doctrine. The imagery of gangrene in this verse provides another such contrast – the Pastoral Epistles repeatedly speak of 'sound doctrine', a lovely term that identifies scripturally correct teaching as both healthy and health-giving. The image is altogether antithetical to that found in this verse. The spreading stench and decay of gangrene, and its disastrous consequences, not only for the affected limb but for the whole person, were much more familiar to Timothy and his contemporaries that they are to us. It does not, however, require a very vivid imagination to appreciate how disgusting and how dangerous the condition was in a world without antibiotics. It is this image that the apostle uses to convey the true character of this false teaching – 'their word will eat as doth a canker'. The term alerts us, not just to the fact that this teaching is dangerous, but also to the fact that it is defiling and destructive – it grows by consuming (literally by finding pasture, the same word is used in Jn 10:9).

Paul then warns Timothy of two false teachers who exemplify this danger. Of Hymenaeus and Philetus we know almost nothing – Hymenaeus is presumably the same individual mentioned in 1 Timothy 1:20, and Philetus is mentioned only here. They are mentioned here as examples of those 'who have swerved from the truth' (*ESV*). There is a deliberate contrast with Timothy's responsibility to cut a straight line – these men missed the mark and veered off course. And what makes this divergence so serious is that they have erred 'concerning the truth'. Their error was not a superficial one, no mere matter of presentation. Right at the heart of the matter they had gone wrong, swerving not from any merely human standard, but from 'the truth'.

Their divergence from the truth was expressed in their 'saying that the resurrection is past already'. Why they were saying this, and what exactly they meant by it has been the subject of considerable – and inconclusive – scholarly debate.[65] For whatever reason, and in response to whatever influence, Hymenaeus and Philetus were suffering from what is sometimes called an 'over-realised eschatology'.[66] It is likely that they were teaching that the resurrection of the believer was a purely spiritual experience, and denying the reality of a future physical resurrection. This teaching did not, by any means, die with Hymenaeus and Philetus, and even though the specific false teaching that they were propagating is no longer commonplace, the fundamental elements of their error are hardly extinct. Hymenaeus and Philetus took what is future, and taught that it had already happened. They took what is literal, and taught that it was spiritual and figurative.[67] They may not actually have been amillennialists, but their approach to Scripture is alarmingly similar.

Whatever the fine detail of the false teaching, it suffices us to realise that it missed the mark of truth – and that its consequences were serious. Again, the issue was not so much that Hymenaeus and Philetus had erred

---

[65] Helpfully summarized in Towner, *Timothy*, 526–8 and, on the wider question of false teachers in the Pastoral Epistles, Witherington III, *Letters*, 341–347.
[66] Fee, *1 & 2 Timothy*, 256. Luke Timothy Johnson, *Letters to Paul's Delegates: 1 Timothy, 2 Timothy, Titus*, The New Testament in Context, (Harrisburg, PA: Trinity Press International, 1996), 75 calls it 'an acute realized eschatology'.
[67] I owe this point to David Gilliland, Bible reading on 2 Timothy 2, Larne Conference, 2016.

themselves – the bigger problem was the impact that their teaching had on others. As believers imbibed the profane babbling of Hymenaeus and Philetus, their faith was overthrown – a word that is closely related to the one used to describe the upending of the moneychangers' tables in John 2:15. 'Hymenaeus and Philetus were not just misdirected doctrinally but were functioning as a two-man wrecking crew of the fragile faith of first-generation believers under Timothy's care.'[68]

As we approach the end of this section, three observations are worth making. Firstly, it is striking how dynamic the language in these verses is – we have 'cutting a straight line', turning our backs, progress (in a bad sense), swerving, missing the mark, and being overthrown. While there are places in Scripture where we are told to stand fast (e.g., 1 Cor. 16:13, Eph. 6:13, 14, 2 Thess. 2:15), there is no thought of immobility or stasis in these verses. We are moving – in the right direction or the wrong, but moving in any case. The practical implication is clear – our relationship with the Word of God should not – and cannot – be a static thing. We should be moving ever forward in our understanding of the truth of God's Word. We should be active in turning away from that which is unprofitable. If we do not, we are in danger of spiralling downwards into ever increasing ungodliness, missing the mark of truth like a poorly aimed arrow.

The second thing that is evident in these verses is the importance of truth. We live in a society that queries – and more often denies – the existence of absolute truth. In its absence, everything is relative, and all we can do is quibble about meaning. But these verses make it clear that there is an objective standard – it is not for nothing that verse 15 speaks of 'the word of truth' or that it is

---

[68] Yarbrough, *The Letters to Timothy and Titus*, 389.

'concerning the truth' that Hymenaeus and Philetus have erred. This has vital implications for our approach to Scripture – we should never come to God's Word to find hooks to hang our own opinions on, but to seek diligently and dependently to understand what Scripture actually says. And, if we are to teach as Timothy taught, the purpose of our ministry will be to help our listeners to grasp the objective truth of the Word of God.

Thirdly, it is worth noting, once more, the unrelenting focus in this section on the consequences of teaching. Those consequences are personal to the person doing the teaching – shame awaits the workman who is not approved by God – but the main stress is on the wider, congregational, consequences of teaching. Teaching, in these verses, is either beneficial or baneful – there is little thought of middle ground. Two important practical implications follow from this. These verses justify us in evaluating doctrine by extrapolating it to its practical consequence. In other words, when we encounter a line of biblical teaching for the first time, we are wise to ask 'where will this lead?' or 'what sort of behaviour is this likely to produce?' If a line of doctrine seems likely to produce behaviour that is ungodly, then we can be pretty certain that it is not in accord with the word of truth, but, rather, is something on which we should turn our backs. Consequences, however, are not just a metric for the teaching of others. Those of us who teach the people of God need always to have before us the blessing of the saints. This should be the primary motivation any time we open our mouths. Not the display of our knowledge, the advancement of an agenda, or the desire to be heard, but the benefit of God's people should be the goal at which we aim. To do otherwise is to hazard the spiritual stability of our hearers, and to store up shame for the judgement seat of Christ.

Verse 19a 'Nevertheless the foundation of God standeth sure.' Like a thunderclap or a trumpet blast this affirmation rings out from the pages of Scripture. Regardless of the profane and vain babblings, the gangrenous false teaching, and the catastrophic error outlined in the previous verses, the foundation of God stands sure. Above all the movement that we have seen in this section – the cutting of a straight line in a positive sense, the overthrowing and downward progression of error and swerving from the truth in a negative sense – God's foundation stands, unmoved and unmovable, steadfast and reliable. Paul had warned Timothy about the devastating consequences of false teaching. But in spite of the very real dangers, Timothy had no need to despair for he could be assured that, no matter what the attack, 'God's solid foundation remains standing' (NET).

Paul does not explicitly identify 'God's solid foundation'. The expression has, among other things, been understood as a reference to the Person of Christ, to the certainty of God's ultimate triumph, to the church in Ephesus, or to the Church in the wider, dispensational sense.[69] Others have argued that it is impossible or, at any rate, undesirable to tie the expression to a single meaning – William Kelly, for example, argues that 'there seems no sufficient ground for defining the foundation in this place. If the Holy Spirit has left it general, why should any seek to limit the thought?'[70] This lack of unanimity should make one proceed with caution, and Kelly's point carries a good deal of weight. Notwithstanding this, in light of the

---

[69] Towner, *Timothy*, 530.
[70] Kelly, *Exposition*, 230.

immediate context of the verse and the ways in which Paul uses the word 'foundation' in Romans 15:20, 1 Corinthians 3:10, and Ephesians 2:20, it is, perhaps, surprising that more interpreters have not seen here a reference to the Word of God, and particularly the truth outlined in verses 8–13 of the chapter. In a scene marked by doctrinal conflict and corruption, what Timothy needs assurance about is that the truth – the Word of God – cannot be affected by the onslaught of error. It has stood and keeps on standing, as the perfect tense asserts. This interpretation might well be said to embrace the others, for Christ, the church, and the triumph of God's kingdom are all revealed in Scripture, and if it stands, they stand too.[71]

Excursus The implications of understanding 'the foundation of God' as a reference to Scripture are worth teasing out a little, for they are immensely relevant to the context in which we find ourselves. Doing so will require me to trespass upon the reader's endurance with a brief philosophical excursus which, happily, can be avoided by skipping to the end of the paragraph. Since about the 1960s, postmodern philosophy has permeated western thought. Originating in the universities of France, it has spread well beyond the boundaries of academia to infect and affect philosophy and education to the extent that it has become the default mode of thought even for those happy souls who have never heard of Barthes, Derrida, or Foucault. One of the more influential claims of postmodernism is the idea that meaning can never be finally determined, so that there is no such thing as

---

[71] The comparison with 1 Corinthians 3 is instructive here. The view that 'God's sure foundation' is Christ typically appeals to 1 Cor. 3:11. But, as verse 10 makes clear, the foundation is Christ as revealed in the teaching of the apostle – in our context, in the Word of God.

absolute truth. This idea has problematic implications in all sorts of areas, but for our present purposes, its impact on the interpretation of texts is particularly important. It implies that the final meaning of a text cannot be fixed, that there is, in fact, no such thing as a final meaning or a correct understanding of a text. Every reader is free to construct his or her own meaning – indeed that is all the reader is able to do. Applied to literary texts, this approach has had the relatively harmless side-effect of keeping literary critics busy, allowing them never to have to agree with each other. It has also not been altogether without benefit in reminding us that objective interpretation of texts is very difficult and that our efforts to understand texts are far more informed by our cultural context and presuppositions than we might imagine. The problem arises, however, when this philosophy – which most of us have unconsciously imbibed – affects our understanding of Scripture. Instead of asking 'what does this passage mean?' we begin to ask 'what does this passage mean *for me?*', and we abandon any attempt at objectivity for a wholehearted embrace of subjectivity. To this tendency, this verse stands as a powerful corrective. 'The foundation of God is steadfast'. It has an objective existence that is no more touched by the swervings and squabblings of false teachers than Nelson's Column by the scurryings of an ant. Like Timothy, we must be diligent to rightly divide the word of truth, but whether we succeed or not, God's foundation still stands steadfast.

Verse 19b To move from foundations to seals may seem to us to be a mixing of metaphors – we associate seals with documents, rather than buildings. 'The metaphor is based on the practice of inscribing a seal on the foundation of a building in order to indicate ownership and sometimes the function of a building.'[72] In the context, we would more usually use 'inscription', but 'seal' has additional connotations of authority, ownership, and authenticity. The seal on God's foundation combines two statements. The first, 'The Lord knoweth them that are His', is a quotation from Numbers 16:5.[73] That passage refers to the judgement of Korah and demonstrates God's ability to defend His truth by judging those who rise up against it. The second, 'Let every one that nameth the name of Christ depart from iniquity', has been identified as an allusion to a whole range of Old Testament passages, including, most persuasively Leviticus 24:16 or Isaiah 26:13.[74] Both of these passages refer to 'naming the name' of the Lord – in blasphemy in Leviticus 24:26 and in identification and acknowledgement in Isaiah 26:13. While it might be tempting to see a second reference to the Pentateuch and to Divine judgement here, a reference to Isaiah 26:13 seems to better fit the context.

Identifying the possible sources of these quotations is of only limited help in understanding what they mean in this passage. The context of the passage is vital here – Paul has been dealing with false teachers and false teaching. In the first part of this seal, he draws a line of demarcation between false teachers and true. The statement is positive – that the Lord knows those that are His is a precious truth and an encouragement to our souls. In light of the background of Numbers 16, however, 'the statement is used primarily in a negative

---

[72] Mounce, *Pastoral Epistles*, 529
[73] An exact quotation from the Septuagint (LXX), except that 'God' has been altered to 'Lord'.
[74] See Towner, *Timothy*, 532–536, but see Mounce, *Pastoral Epistles*, 530, who argues that 'most of the passages suggested as possible sources seem at best to be remote possibilities.'

fashion to show that the Lord will exclude those whom He does not recognise as His people'.[75] God will judge false teachers in the mould of Hymenaeus and Philetus, just as surely as He dealt with rebels like Korah, Dathan, and Abiram. The change in Divine title (from God to Lord) compared to the LXX serves to underscore His sovereign authority – He is the Lord, and He knows those that belong to Him.

The second half of the seal develops the implication of the first. Those who name the name of Christ must withdraw from iniquity. They must depart from it, just as the Israelites were instructed to 'depart ... from the tents of these wicked men' (Num. 16:26).[76] In the widest sense, it is, of course, true that those who name the name of Christ, those who are identified with Him and who call upon Him, should withdraw from all that is unrighteous and evil. But, in the context of this passage, Paul is making a much more specific point. There is doctrinal, as well as moral evil, and one is as serious as the other. It is to doctrinal evil, specifically that Paul is referring here. False teaching is not to be tolerated; those who name the name of Christ are to withdraw, not just from false teaching, but from false teachers as well.

The fact that seals are usually linked with the concept of authentication suggests that there may be an additional layer of meaning here. Timothy can be sure that the Lord knows those – in the context, those teachers – who are genuine. The first half of the seal says as much, and this guarantees that the false teachers will, in God's time, be judged. But God's people, too, need to be able to distinguish the true from the false. And because they do not share God's knowledge of who is His and who is not, they must rely on other evidence. If

---

[75] Marshall, *Pastoral Epistles*, 756.
[76] The LXX uses a form of the same verb (*aphistēmi*) here.

they encountered a teacher who named the name of Christ, but who did not depart from evil, they could be sure that his ministry was not authentic, not built on the foundation, but corrupt and corrupting. 'Ye shall know them by their fruits' (Mt. 7:16) was the principle outlined by the Lord Jesus, and it applied in Timothy's day no less than in ours.

vv. 20, 21   Sanctification

From the metaphor of a foundation in verse 19, Paul moves to the image of a 'great house'. It is important to note that, while the two images share an architectural metaphor and make the same central point, they are two separate images – there is neither need nor justification for making the foundation the foundation of the great house, and to do so tends to complicate and confuse what is, taken on its own terms, 'an everyday, commonsense analogy'.[77]

The picture is also confused by the suggestion that 'a great house' should be interpreted as a picture of the Church,[78] the local church,[79] or of Christendom (sometimes termed 'the visible Church').[80] The third suggestion need not detain us long, for the New Testament knows no such concept as Christendom or 'the visible Church'. Superficially, the idea that 'a great house' might refer to the Church might seem more

---

[77] Yarbrough, *Letters to Timothy and Titus*, 393. In fact, as we noted previously, a number of commentators conflate the two, arguing that both the foundation and the building are to be identified as the Church – a rather approximate and unsatisfactory approach that hardly does justice to the imagery of the passage.
[78] See, for a detailed discussion and defence of this view, Gregory A. Couser, '"How Firm a Foundation": The Ecclesiology of 2 Timothy 2:19–21', *Bibliotheca Sacra*, 173, 460–475.
[79] Wall, *1 & 2 Timothy and Titus*, 255.
[80] MacDonald, *Believer's Bible Commentary*, 2118, Hendriksen, *I–II Timothy and Titus*, 270.

persuasive, for 1 Timothy 3:15 does describe the church of the living God as 'house of God'. On closer examination, however, this argument is unconvincing – firstly because the house of God in 1 Timothy is the local assembly and not the Church, the body of Christ, and secondly because the word for house that is used here is different from that used in 1 Timothy. The word used here (*oikia*) refers to the physical structure of the house, while the term used in 1 Timothy (*oikos*) refers rather to 'the social household reality'.[81] This is also an issue for those who wish to see the local church as the 'great house'. The case for seeing the Church, in either its universal or local aspect, in the verse is, then, flimsy, even before reckoning with the additional and unnecessary exegetical complexities that result from overinterpreting the analogy.

'A great house', then, is just that – it is literally a large dwelling, an actual, physical house. And in any great house there will be vessels of different materials, designed for different purposes. These vessels are classified in two different ways. The first classification is based on the material that the vessels are made from – Paul lists four types of vessel, divided into two sets of two – vessels of gold and silver and vessels of wood and earth. The second has to do with use – some vessels are for noble purposes, others for ignoble. This much is clear and uncontested. However, there is considerable disagreement among commentators about if and how the two classifications interact with each other. Some see the two classifications as parallel. Vessels of gold and silver, they argue, are vessels to honour, vessels of wood and earth are vessels to dishonour. This view is informed by the presence in these verses of three materials that are also mentioned in 1 Corinthians 3:12, and effectively

[81] Towner, *Timothy*, 537.

imports Paul's teaching in that passage into his argument here. The difficulty with this is that Paul is making a very different point in this passage, and trying to shoehorn the teaching of 1 Corinthians 3 into this chapter obscures Paul's argument and introduces all manner of loose ends, in a way that should alert us to the fact that our interpretation has gone astray somehow.

Indeed, simply moving our eye into verse 21 is sufficient to confirm that this reading has missed the point. It is cleanliness that determines whether a vessel is to honour or to dishonour – a purged vessel is fit for a noble purpose, even if it is made of wood or earth. Similarly, a vessel that is not clean is fit only for an ignoble purpose, even if it is crafted from gold and silver. In a great house all sorts of vessels are needed – wood and earth are just as vital as gold and silver. Each has its purpose, each is 'useful for the Master' – so long as it is clean. Not everyone can be a vessel of gold and silver but it is open to everyone to be a vessel to honour – a point emphasised by the indefinite pronoun that the KJV translates as 'a man', but which might better be rendered 'anyone', as it is in many translations. This is the key point of the image and it is simple enough if we allow the passage to speak to us on its own terms.

It is less straightforward to identify what cleansing exactly Paul has in mind. The verse literally says 'if anyone cleanse himself from these', without specifying what 'these' refers to. A glance at the translations indicates the range of possible identifications – the NIV has 'from the latter', the dishonourable vessels of verse 20, the ESV 'what is dishonorable', the CSB 'anything dishonorable', the NET 'such behaviour', and the NRSV 'the things I have mentioned'. Further examples could be multiplied, but they divide into two main categories – either the verse is referring to the false teachers or it is referring to their teaching and its corrupting consequences. There is little to choose between the two interpretations, provided that we do not lose sight of the fact that it is still doctrinal evil that is primarily in view – Paul will address the need for moral cleanliness in the following verses – or the implication that Timothy is to withdraw from false teachers personally as well as from 'the doctrines and deeds of Hymenaeus and Philetus and their followers'.[82]

By thoroughly cleansing[83] himself of the defilement of the false teachers and their doctrine, Timothy would ensure that he was a 'vessel unto honour'. What is involved in being a 'vessel unto honour' is unpacked in the three expressions that follow – it means to be sanctified, useful to the Master, and 'prepared unto every good work'. To be sanctified is to be set apart as holy; devoted to God's service. To be set apart like this is to be 'meet for the Master's use. There is a contrast here with the uselessness of the false teachers (Paul uses a related word to describe their profitless strivings in v. 14b). 'Prepared unto every good work' sounds a characteristic note in the Pastoral Epistles, where repeated reference is made to 'good works'. The vessel unto honour is to be useful, not just to God, but to man as well, standing ready to undertake good (that is, beautiful and beneficial) works. Paul works from the inside out – inner sanctification guarantees usefulness for God and good works to our fellow man. Doctrinal purity is no arid academic matter – it is a prerequisite of a profitable Christian life.

It must be acknowledged that the understanding of these verses outlined in this article is decidedly a

---

[82] Yarbrough, *Letters to Timothy and Titus*, 393.
[83] The verb is used elsewhere in the NT only in 1 Cor. 5:7 ('purge out the old leaven').

minority one. Few commentators can resist the urge to see 'a great house' as a figure to be interpreted, though they tend to expend more ingenuity in interpreting the figure than in establishing that it is there to be interpreted in the first place.[84] This assumption occasions a great deal of complexity in interpreting who the vessels are, what it means to be a vessel unto honour or dishonour, whether the false teachers are vessels or not, and a great many other issues besides. The fact that there is no consensus about the answers to these questions should serve as a further warning that something has gone awry in the interpretation of the passage. Moreover, these discussions tend to lose sight of the central – and simple – point that Paul is making, which is that a failure on the part of Timothy to eschew the false teachers and their doctrine would, inevitably, prevent him from being useful to God as a vessel of honour. Simple the point may be, but it is no less solemn for all that. I may be a vessel of gold or silver. I may be a vessel of wood or earth, with a role to play that is no less vital. But if I am to be used for noble purposes I must be clean – and so, fellow Christian, must you.

vv. 22–26   **Service**

Verse 22 The preposition *de* ('but' or 'and', translated 'also' by the KJV here) at the beginning of verse 22 signals a move to a new, though related, subject. In parallel with the structure of verses 14–16, this section contains three

---

[84] Couser, 'How Firm an Foundation' is a good, though by no means unusual, example of this. The 'ecclesial nature of the metaphor' is asserted in two sentences, but pages are devoted to untangling the exegetical knots that have only been tied because of the assumption that the house is the Church. A number of commentators appeal to their understanding of the foundation of verse 19 as the Church (e.g., Towner, *Timothy*, 537), but this conflation of a foundation with the building that is built on it seems to be more a problem with, than a proof of, their argument.

imperatives – 'flee', 'follow', 'avoid' – following the pattern negative, positive, negative.

Having urged Timothy to 'purge himself' from false teachers without, Paul urges him to 'flee ... youthful lusts' within. The imperative 'flee' is one that Paul uses on several occasions: regarding fornication (1 Cor. 6:18), idolatry (1 Cor. 10:14), and the 'love of money' and the overmastering desire to be rich (1 Tim. 6:11). Here the instruction is to 'seek safety by flight'[85] from 'youthful passions' (NET, ESV, etc.). Although the word 'lusts' tends to make us automatically think of illicit sexual desire, the word in the original simply means 'desire'. Desire can be positive as well as negative (*cf.* Lk. 22:15, Phil. 1:23), and we can only determine what is being desired, and whether it is good or bad, from the context. Clearly the 'youthful lusts' that Paul has in mind here are not positive. Given the verses that follow, he seems to have in view, not so much questions of personal morality, as an obstinate or argumentative spirit, an assertive and arrogant demeanour, and a love of controversy – 'self-assertion as well as self-indulgence'.[86] These vices are not the sole domain of the young, but, without the mollifying effect of age and experience, they do, perhaps, present a greater temptation. Given what we are told elsewhere of Timothy's character and temperament, 'the reference here is almost certainly not to his own tendencies but to those evident in the church, and especially among the troublemakers.'[87] But even

---

[85] *Pheugō*, William F. Arndy and F. Wilbur Gingrich, *A Greek-English Lexicon of the New Testament and Other Early Chrisitan Literature*, (Chicago, IL: University of Chicago Press, 20010, *s.v.* The word is used of the flight of Joseph and Mary to Egypt (Mt. 2:13), of the flight of the disciples from Gethsemane (Mk. 14:50), and by the Lord in His warning to the Pharisees to 'flee from the wrath to come' (Mt. 3:7).

[86] Walter Lock, *The Pastoral Epistles*, International Critical Commentary, (Edinburgh: T&T Clark, 1924), 101.

[87] Towner, *Timothy*, 543.

Timothy, in an atmosphere of controversy and opposition, needed to be aware of the danger of succumbing to these youthful lusts, for even the mildest of us are not immune from their temptation given the right combination of circumstances.

Timothy is not only to flee; he is also to follow. In a number of places, the word translated 'follow' is translated 'persecute' (e.g., Mt. 5:10, 11; Jn 5:16, 20; Acts 9:4 etc.). The last of the examples cited was used by the risen Lord Jesus to Paul on the road to Damascus. There, Paul was arrested in no half-hearted searching after Christians – he was pursuing them vigorously and with zeal, to the exclusion of all else. With such energy and such determination Timothy was to pursue 'righteousness, faith, charity, peace'. The first three virtues mentioned here also appear in 1 Timothy 6:11, but Paul is emphasising the virtues that are particularly important to Timothy's context, not just reeling off a standard list. 'Righteousness' (*dikaiosynē*) stands in contrast to the 'iniquity', or unrighteousness (*adikia*) of verse 19. This righteousness is to issue in a right relationship with God – 'faith' – and with man – 'love'. These elements, in their proper place, will produce the final item in the list – an item which does not appear in 1 Timothy 6:11 or Paul's other, similar, lists of virtues. Timothy must persecute peace. He must not, as the following verses make clear, promote or participate in strife. But the peace that Paul is speaking of is not the pseudo-peace that is produced by failing to teach the truth or by allowing error to pass unopposed. Timothy is to pursue peace, but only along the road that leads first through righteousness, to faith, and then to love. And he will not travel alone. Rather, as he follows this route, he will find himself in the company of 'them that call on the Lord out of a pure heart'. This beautiful description of believers echoes and exemplifies the language of the second part of the seal (v. 19). True Christianity is not just external profession (calling on the Lord) it is also an inward condition 'out of a pure heart'. This emphasis upon the communal element of Christianity acts as an encouraging counterpoint to the purging of verse 21. It would have been possible for Timothy – as it is for us – to go to extremes and to become isolated and suspicious. The end of this verse calls us back to the reality that, although there are false teachers who must be shunned and avoided, there are also true believers in whose company and with whose fellowship we can pursue peace.

Verse 23 Timothy is to 'flee' and to 'follow', and now, to 'avoid'. The 'questions' – 'arguments' (*NIV*), 'controversies' (*ESV, NET*), 'speculations' (*NASB*) – are not genuine queries (which should never be unwelcome), but rather debating points, lumped, in 1 Timothy 6:4, with 'strifes of words'. It is likely that few of us have difficulty in illustrating the point by reference to our own experience. The futility of these controversies is underlined by the fact that they are 'foolish and unlearned'. Foolish 'describes the verbal wrangling as frivolous and unskilled because it produces nothing useful'.[88] Unlearned means uneducated – a characterisation that ironically underscores the emptiness of the false teachers' pretensions.[89] And, lest there be any lingering trace of doubt, Paul points to the outcome of these controversies – they 'produce quarrels'. In an epistle where the focus has been so firmly on what is produced by teaching, the indictment is damning.

---

[88] Towner, *Timothy*, 545.
[89] The Greek word used is *apaideutosi*, which occurs only here in the NT. *Paideutosi* comes from a word group that has to do with instruction and education, which is negated by the prefix.

These pointless quibblings produce nothing of value – they serve only to foster disagreement and bickering.

It is striking and sobering how relevant the teaching of this verse is. Likely all of us will have taken part in conversations composed of 'foolish and unlearned questions'. Some of us will have experienced teaching that matches this description. Perhaps some of us have given it. Not for nothing does Paul speak about 'lusts'. Debating fine points appeals to the flesh in many of us and too often we fail to obey the apostle's teaching and indulge in profitless speculation that, whether it takes place around the tea table or from the platform, issues ultimately in raised tempers, unkind words, and strife. This is not, by any means, to suggest that all discussion of the Scripture is wrong – would that there were more of it and that our conversation were less occupied with the ephemera of the everyday. But may we seek, with God's help, always to ensure that we are discussing issues of substance in a way that will be profitable, not seeking the pseudo-intellectual satisfaction of chewing on old chestnuts and points of controversy that raise the hearer's blood pressure but not his spirituality.

Verse 24 Strife is flatly incompatible with what it means to be 'the servant of the Lord' – the 'but' which begins the verse emphasises the contrast as does the deliberate echo in 'gender strifes ... must not strive'. Nor does the language of obligation – 'must not strive' – leave any room for doubt. 'The servant of the Lord' is a title that emphasises both responsibility and dignity. But although it is a title of dignity, it conveys no entitlement to arrogance. Quite the opposite – there is an obligation upon the servant of God to be marked by gentleness, meekness, and patience. Paul uses the word translated 'gentle' twice – here and in 1 Thessalonians 2:7. The latter verse demonstrates the scope of what he has in mind: 'we were gentle among you, like a nursing mother taking care of her own children' (ESV). There is to be no partiality in how that gentleness is to be displayed – it is 'unto all', not just Timothy's friends or co-defenders of the truth, but even his most implacable and obdurate opponents were to be treated kindly. There is, however, no thought that this gentleness would restrict the proclamation of the truth, for the gentle servant of God must also be 'apt to teach'. To our ear, 'apt to teach' sounds like 'willing to teach', but it means more than that – Timothy must be both willing and able to teach. And he must be patient. Patience is essential for any teaching, most of all when those you are trying to teach are opposed both to you and your message. The word that is used here (and only here in the New Testament), though, means something more than just patience – it involves being 'patient of ills and wrongs'[90] and 'envisions a capacity for tolerance (of insults, contradiction) in the face of opposition'.[91]

Verse 25 The focus now moves from what the servant of the Lord must be, to what he must do. The keynote here, emphasised by the structure of the sentence, is meekness.[92] Meekness, or gentleness born of humility, must be the hallmark of Timothy's approach to 'those that oppose themselves'. Verses 25 and 26 explain why. The correction and recovery of the false teachers is no merely human endeavour. If it were, the force of Timothy's personality, his facility in argument, and his ability to outwit or overwhelm his opponents might

---

[90] Thayer, *Greek Lexicon, s.v.*
[91] Towner, *Timothy*, 547.
[92] 'The placement of the prepositional phrase ahead of the participle it governs is emphatic'. (Towner, *Timothy*, 547, n. 153).

have had some relevance. But this is not, as these verses make very clear, a merely human matter. 'Those that oppose themselves' are in 'the snare of the devil', 'taken captive by him at his will' (v. 26), needing God to 'give them repentance'. They require, not to be overpowered by a forceful personality, but to receive Divine deliverance from a supernatural power. Timothy's appreciation of his smallness in contrast to this far vaster spiritual picture would produce meekness, and our appreciation that, as servants of the Lord we are only a very small part of something far bigger should do the same. It should not paralyse us – Timothy was still to instruct the false teachers – but it should wring from us any trace of arrogance or self-confidence.

Timothy's instruction, then, takes its place in a far larger context of spiritual conflict. But it does have a place. The word 'instruction', or education, picks up on Paul's use of a negative form of the same word in the phrase 'unlearned questions' in verse 23. Timothy is to hold himself from uneducated controversies and is instead to seek to instruct 'those that oppose themselves'. This expression is used only here. The KJV translation might give the impression that Paul is speaking of those who oppose their own best interests (and that is true). However, the implication is more far-ranging and serious than this. These opponents have 'set themselves in opposition' – to Timothy, yes, but, far more seriously, to God and to His truth.

Paul does not make it explicit whether these opponents are the false teachers, those who have been led astray by the false teachers, or both. In light of the language used in verse 26, however, it seems likely that it is the false teachers themselves who are in view. Their condition is serious, but it is not altogether hopeless. There is a possibility that Timothy's attempts to instruct them will be successful, but it is by no means guaranteed. Paul's use of a 'weak interrogative particle'[93] means that 'a positive outcome is entertained [but] the idiom couches it in very cautious terms'.[94] But, if their rescue is to be accomplished, it requires Divine action – that God 'will give them repentance to the acknowledging of the truth'. On three occasions in the New Testament, we read of God granting repentance – to the Jews (Acts 5:31), to the Gentiles (Acts 11:18), and in this passage. None of these passages contemplates any sort of overriding of human responsibility, but each emphasises Divine grace in allowing human beings to hear and to respond to His Word. Here, the goal of Timothy's patient instruction is that the opponents would be brought, by way of repentance, to 'the acknowledging of the truth'. Coming 'to the knowledge of the truth' is linked with salvation in 1 Timothy 2:4, though it is not clear that the terms are intended to be synonymous (as many commentators argue). In the context of this passage, it is difficult to say dogmatically whether these false teachers are unsaved men who need to come 'to the knowledge of the truth' in salvation, or whether they are believers whose defective grasp of the Word of God needs to be corrected. On balance, and notwithstanding the solemnity of the language used in verse 26, the second possibility is perhaps more likely.

Verse 26 makes the full extent of the false teachers' plight pitilessly clear. They are intoxicated and enslaved, mere tools of the devil. 'That they may recover themselves' means "to return to soberness", as from a

---

[93] Mounce, *Pastoral Epistles*, 536.
[94] Towner, *Timothy*, 548.

state of delirium or drunkenness'.[95] False teaching has already been depicted as a gangrenous disease, destroying what it feeds on. Here it is presented as a stupefying narcotic, an intoxicant that produces a moral and intellectual senselessness. These unhappy individuals need to be summoned from their stupor. They also need to be delivered from the 'snare' or trap of the devil, an expression that Paul also uses in 1 Timothy 3:7. Those who have swerved from the truth (v. 18) have chosen a dangerous course – they have, all unknowing, wandered into Satan's snare and have been 'taken captive by him at his will'.

This expression has given rise to much discussion about who has done the capturing and at whose will.[96] Paul's use of pronouns means that either God or Satan could be in view in each case and some interpreters have argued that the verse is speaking about the capture of the false teachers by God out of Satan's snare so that they might do His will. Though this is possible, it is more probable that Paul is adding a further solemn detail about the predicament of these men – Satan has captured them, so that they might do his will.

These verses bring the chapter to a solemn close. Timothy could be under no illusion about the task that lay before him. In this context, it was no light thing to be 'the servant of the Lord', and no simple thing to be a 'workman that needeth not to be ashamed'. But Timothy must be both, and so must we. And, in spite of every discouraging circumstance, we can do so firm in the confidence that God abides faithful and that His foundation stands sure.

---

[95] W.E. Vine, *Vine's Expository Dictionary of New Testament Words*, (London: Oliphants, 1963), s.v.
[96] See Towner, *Timothy*, 549-551 for a detailed discussion.

Chapter Three

3:1–17   The awareness of the man of God

vv. 1–9   **The Fierceness of the Times**

AT THE END OF CHAPTER 2, the apostle reminded Timothy that the local and immediate difficulties that he was experiencing in Ephesus had, as their background, a much larger and more far-reaching context – the efforts of Satan to oppose and overthrow the work of God. As we move into chapter 3, the apostle continues to fill in the background, to locate Timothy's service not just in the context of satanic opposition but in the context of 'last days'. As the chapter opens, he begins a series of stern warnings that will run down to the end of verse 9. These verses contain a single instruction to Timothy as to how he is to respond to the challenge of these individuals, but their focus is almost entirely on their character (vv. 1–4), their conduct (vv. 5–7), and their corruption and ultimate condemnation (vv. 8, 9). The emphatic 'but thou' at the start of verse 10 not only marks the beginning of a new section, it also moves the focus back to Timothy: the background recedes once more into shadow as the spotlight of Divine revelation concentrates again on Paul, Timothy, and 'all that will live godly in Christ Jesus' (v. 12).

Verse 1 The importance and urgency of what Paul has to say in these verses is emphasised by the opening imperative 'this know'. This calls Timothy not just to be aware of the information that Paul was about to impart, but to accept it and to understand its implications. Paul wants Timothy to grasp the character of 'last days'. This term, which is fundamental to our understanding of the passage, has been interpreted in a number of ways. Some commentators suggest that the 'last days' refers to a specific period at the end of the dispensation of grace when sudden and accelerating decline sets in, and which leads directly to the return of Christ and the judgement of the Tribulation.[1] This view, however, seems somewhat anomalous in light of the general New Testament usage of the expression 'last days'. Acts 2:17 and Hebrews 1:2 both use the term to describe the period that commenced with the first advent of Christ and the descent of the Spirit. Peter uses the similar expression 'last times' in 1 Peter 1:20, again with the whole dispensation in view. It is also significant that the instruction to Timothy, in verse 5, to 'turn away' from men of the character outlined in these verses suggests – even if it does not definitively prove – that Paul sees Timothy as living in 'last days'. It is worth noting that the expression 'last days' is anarthrous (i.e., it does not have an article, it is 'last days', not 'the last days'). This means that the emphasis is on the character of these days, rather than on their chronology. Timothy, like us, served God in 'last days' and Timothy, like us, needed to understand that the character of those days provided the context for his service.

---

[1] See, for example, Thomas Ice, 'Are We Living in the Last Days?' (2009), https://digitalcommons.liberty.edu/pretrib.arch/61/, 'the Bible ... warns about some general trends toward the later part of the church age'. See also Baker, *II Timothy*, 359, 360.

That context was a difficult and dangerous one for, in last days, 'perilous times shall come'. Despite what the KJV rendering might suggest, the thought here is probably not of an irreversible moment of decline that happens at some future point. Rather – as suggested by the translation in the NIV ('There will be terrible times in the last days') and JND ('difficult times shall be there') – the idea is that perilous times will be endemic in last days. 'What Timothy is to understand about the last days is not that they are uniformly, continuously evil, but that they will include "perilous seasons".'[2] 'Perilous' leaves us in no doubt about just how difficult these times will be – the word is used elsewhere in the New Testament only in Matthew 8:28, where it describes the two demon-possessed men from the country of the Gergesenes who were 'exceeding fierce'. The word translated 'times' (*kairos*) emphasises character, rather than chronology – Paul is providing a canvas, not a calendar.

Verse 2 What will make these times terrible will be the character of the people who operate in them. While the temptation to read these verses as a denouncement of society as a whole is real, the fact that they have 'a form of godliness, but [deny] the power thereof' along with the instruction to Timothy to turn from these people (v. 5) suggests that Paul has in view specifically those who have professed to be believers. That is confirmed by the number of items in the list that follows that appear in Romans 1 (and sometimes only there, outside of this passage). The vices outlined in these verses are unremarkable – though distressing – in society as a whole; they can always be observed, rather than being a

---

[2] Fee, *1 & 2 Timothy*, 83.

marker of 'perilous times'. Evidence of them among those who profess to be – and to teach – believers, however, is a different matter altogether.

The list of vices presented in verses 2 to 5 is daunting. That is its primary purpose: 'Paul's intention is not to unravel the chemistry of impurity in a precise way. ... The list intends to create a broad impact upon its readers.'[3] There has been much debate about the way in which the items listed are arranged, and even on how many vices are listed.[4] The variety displayed in attempts to group the items on the list into categories or to identify a relationship between them suggests that these efforts owe more to the ingenuity of the interpreter than to a structure imposed upon them by the apostle. This is not to suggest that the list is random or arbitrary, rather that its organisation is more general than we might like to think. Although this is one of those passages that threatens to lure the expositor into simple and unhelpful (and, worse, tedious) paraphrase, we will need to examine each of the vices listed in a little detail. Before embarking on that examination, however, there are some general points about this list that are worth bearing in mind.

We have already alluded to the first of these. It is striking that five of the terms used here ('boasters', 'proud', 'disobedient to parents', 'without natural affection', and 'trucebreakers') are also found in Paul's indictment of fallen humanity in Romans 1:29–31. That was how Roman society operated and how our own

---

[3] Towner, *Timothy*, 555.
[4] Towner and Fee both identify eighteen items, Baker and Stott nineteen. This variation is not at all consequential: it depends on whether 'lovers of pleasures more than lovers of God' (v. 4) is treated as one item or two or whether 'Having a form of godliness, but denying the power thereof' (v. 5) is treated as an item on the list or (more probably) as a summary of the condition of these men.

society operates. But the times are terrible indeed when these vices, these appetites and attitudes, are found among professing believers and within the local church.

The second striking thing about this list is the way in which it is bracketed by terms including the prefix *phil-* (love). The list opens with 'lovers of their own selves' (*philautos*) and 'covetous' (literally lovers of silver, *philargyros*), and closes with 'lovers of pleasure (*philēdonos*), more than lovers of God (*philotheos*)'. The repeated sounds contribute to the impact of this list, but their repetition is more than poetry. Rather, it emphasises that fact that, in the words of the old cliché, 'the heart of the problem is the problem of the heart'. Fundamental to the spiritual pathology outlined in these verses is misplaced affection, a love, not for God, but for self and for all that ministers to the comfort of self. 'Keep thy heart with all diligence' said Solomon, 'for out of it are the issues of life' (Prov. 4:23), and this list of vices, bracketed by misplaced love, gives grim emphasis to his words.

Thirdly, it is notable that eight of the items on the list begin with the Greek letter α. Again, this alliteration enhances the aural effect of the list but, again, this is more than a stylistic feature. The prefix is an 'alpha privative'. Like the prefix 'un' in English, it expresses negation or absence.[5] In other words, this list is not so much a list of vices as it is a list of missing virtues. Thankfulness, holiness, affection, and so on should all be seen in the lives of believers. Their presence should be unremarkable and their absence appalling. The false teachers whose presence will be a recurring feature of 'last days' are defined by their deficiencies, marked out by what they miss. As we read this list, we should ask

---

[5] English sometimes uses 'a' as a prefix in this way – e.g., atypical, asymmetrical.

whether these missing qualities are seen – as they should be – in our lives.

As we have noted, the bracketing of this vice list with *phil-* words is clearly significant. Other than that, it is difficult to definitively identify an overall organising principle for the list. The items are arranged in fairly approximate pairs, but identifying an overall arc of progression generally seems to reflect the ingenuity of the interpreter rather than a structure intended by the apostle.

With that preamble, it remains briefly to discuss each of the vices listed by the apostle:

Lovers of their own selves (*philautos*) – this word is found only here in the New Testament. This is where everything starts to go wrong in the lives of these individuals. God's standard is 'thou shalt love the Lord thy God with all thy heart, and with all thy soul, and with all thy mind, and with all thy strength ... [and] thou shalt love thy neighbour as thyself' (Mk 12:30, 31), but those greater loves have been displaced by mere and sheer selfishness.

Covetous (*philargyros*) – literally 'lovers of silver'. This word is only found elsewhere in the New Testament in Luke 16:14, where it is used to describe the Pharisees. In that passage, Luke uses the term to explain why the Pharisees were responding with derision to the Lord's teaching 'Ye cannot serve God and mammon.' They thought that they could, and these false teachers were making the same mistake. Paul used the cognate noun when he warned Timothy that 'the love of money is the root of all evil' (1 Tim. 6:10) and so it proves to be here.

Boasters (*alazōn*) – this word occurs elsewhere in the New Testament only in Romans 1:30, as one of the symptoms of humanity's 'reprobate mind'. It is, perhaps, no surprise that those who are selfish and avaricious should be inclined towards 'boistrous, self-aggrandising', and arrogant behaviour.[6] Few of us are immune from the temptation and all of us would do well to emulate Paul in his cry: 'God forbid that I should glory, save in the cross of our Lord Jesus Christ' (Gal. 6:14), and to remember that our blessed Lord, who was 'meek and lowly in heart' (Mt. 11:29), did not 'cry, nor lift up, nor cause His voice to be heard in the street' (Isa. 42:2).

Proud (*hyperēphanos*) – as well as being used in Romans 1:30, this word is found in three other places in the New Testament. Two of these (Jas 4:6; 1 Pet. 5:5) are quotations of Proverbs 3:34: 'God resisteth the proud, but giveth grace unto the humble.' To be proud is to deny God His rightful place in our lives, for pride cannot co-exist with an appreciation of God and of His unmerited and unbounded goodness towards us.

Blasphemers (*blasphēmos*) – this term may mean 'either "blasphemer" of God in a technical religious sense, or more generally "slanderer".'[7] It is likely that Paul intends the more embracive sense here. The wrong attitude to self outlined in the first four items in the list is now being given expression in behaviour and attitudes towards other people. The selfishness of these individuals is manifest in scurrilous and abusive speech, untrammelled by any authority.

Disobedient to parents (*goneusin apeithēs*) – this is the first α-privative in the list. It occurs six times in the New Testament, including in Romans 1. The juxtaposition of this term with the preceding one is one of the factors that suggests that Paul intends blasphemy in the broader sense. Rebellious speech is evidence of a rebellious attitude that reacts against the responsibility of children to obey their parents – one of the most fundamental forms of authority encoded into creation. The point

---

[6] Towner, *Timothy*, 556.
[7] Towner, *Timothy*, 556.

here is not that these people are disobedient to their parents but obedient to other forms of authority; it is, rather, that their disobedience to parents demonstrates their unwillingness to submit to any authority at all.

Unthankful (*acharistos*) – while it is tempting to read this term in the context of familial relationships, Paul is not confining its scope in any way. Rather, this is the general disposition of these individuals – they are marked by an ungracious lack of appreciation. Widely disdained, in the Greek world, 'as being evil and barbaric', it is no more attractive today and utterly unfitting for a Christian. Paul's exhortation to the Colossians was 'be ye thankful' (Col. 3:15) and it is a sad thing if our lives and characters are marked by a deficiency of thankfulness – to God and to our fellow men.

Unholy (*anosios*) – lacking in purity and piety. We tend to stress the first of these, and to think of holiness in terms of freedom from moral contamination. This is certainly an important aspect of holiness. But the term also embraces a 'rejection of sacred norms', the sort of disregard for Divine order that Paul outlines in 1 Timothy 1:9–11.[8] Unholiness is a spiritual state but has important social implications.

Without natural affection (*astorgos*) – found elsewhere only in Romans 1. 'Unloving' (NET, NIV) is a more accurate translation, but the AV's rendering is more eloquent. These individuals are devoid of any affectionate response or warmth towards their fellowman.

Trucebreakers (*aspondos*) – this term is better rendered 'implacable'. The idea is not that they break concords into which they have entered, but that they refuse to form any agreements in the first place. They will not brook any intermission of hostility against their

---

[8] Towner, *Timothy*, 557.

fellowmen. The word 'describes the harshest of attitudes, one that refuses reconciliation and thus leads to the destruction of relationships and lives'.[9]

False accusers (*diabolos*) – Paul breaks the alliteration of this section of the list with a resonant term. In the singular, this can refer to the devil (*cf.* 2:26), but here it describes those who do his work – slandering and maligning others.

Incontinent (*akratēs*) – found only here in the New Testament, this term describes those who lack self-control, who lack the ability to resist temptation or to restrain their appetites. It is a vice that stands in direct opposition to the self-control that is repeatedly identified throughout the Pastoral Epistles as a feature that should mark believers (1 Tim. 3:2; Tit. 1:8; 2:2, 6).

Fierce (*anēmeros*) – found only here in the New Testament, this word, also rendered 'brutal' (ESV, NIV, etc) and 'savage' (NET) describes wild animals, but is used here of those whose brutish behaviour makes them more like animals than men.

Despisers of those that are good (*aphilagathos*) – literally 'not-lovers of good'. Like the *phil-* terms that bracket this list, this term indicates disordered affection. The KJV translation narrows the scope of the expression rather too much – Paul has more in view than just good individuals: he is speaking broadly of everything that is good. Good things, people, and practices should be attractive to Christians (*cf.* Tit.1:8), but they hold no appeal for the individuals in view here.

Traitors (*prodotēs*) – This term occurs on three occasions in the New Testament – it is also used of Judas (Lk. 6:16), the Jews (Acts 7:52), and here, too, it describes betrayers, who break faith and lack any loyalty.

---

[9] Towner, *Timothy*, 557.

Heady (*propetēs*) – 'rash' (NIV), 'reckless' (ESV, NET). The KJV translation, though dated, neatly captures the etymology of this term, which derives from 'falling headlong'. In the Greek translation of the Old Testament, this word occurs in Proverbs 10:14 and 13:3, where the emphasis is on hasty and intemperate speech. In its wider usage, it describes 'hotheaded, impetuous, and overbold acts that end up badly'.[10]

Highminded (*typhoō*) – this term is only found in the epistles to Timothy (1 Tim. 3:6, 6:4). It means being puffed up with, and blinded by, pride.

Lovers of pleasures more than lovers of God (*philēdonoi mallon ē philotheoi*) – with this solemn contrast, Paul brings his list to its climactic conclusion. As at the beginning of the list, so here these individuals are revealed as defective in their love – they love pleasure, and not God. There could hardly be more tragic summary of any man or woman's life.

This list of vices is daunting and depressing. Its primary function for us, as for Timothy, is as a warning – we are being given the distinguishing features of those from whom we must turn. But it would be a mistake to apply this list only externally. Rather, as we read these terrible terms, we should examine our own lives and ask, not just whether these features are absent – as they should be – but whether we possess, in a positive way, those virtues that are so conspicuous by their absence from the lives of these selfish, ferocious, hedonistic people.

Verse 5 In our consideration of 2 Timothy 3:1–4, we have argued that Paul has been describing the conditions that will be manifest among those who claim to be Christians. We have outlined a number of grounds for

---

[10] Towner, *Timothy*, 558.

this view, but none is stronger than this verse's statement that these individuals have 'a form of godliness'. This is a significant expression and deserves careful consideration.

'Godliness' (*eusebeia*) is an important and distinctive concept in the Pastoral Epistles.[11] In Greek culture the term described an attitude of reverence and respect for a range of social institutions and, because the worship of the gods permeated every aspect of society and of life, especially for the gods. However, it was 'its use in Hellenistic Judaism that readied the concept for Pauline use.'[12] Particularly significant in this connection is the use of the word in the Septuagint – the Greek translation of the Old Testament. There it occurs in four passages: Proverbs 1:7 and 13:11, and Isaiah 11:2 and 33:6. In Proverbs 1:7 and the two Isaiah passages, the term is used to translate 'the fear of the Lord', and the two verses from Isaiah also introduce the knowledge of God. In Proverbs 13:11, the emphasis is on righteous behaviour, and the related adjective is used in this sense in a number of passages (Prov. 12:12, 13:19; Isa. 26:7, 32:8). Bringing all this together, then, it is clear that the cliché 'to be godly is to be like God' is, if not inaccurate, at least imprecise. Godliness means living righteously, in a way that is shaped by the revelation of God's character and the reverence that that revelation should produce. Properly speaking, one cannot be truly godly, without knowing God.

---

[11] The noun *eusebeia* occurs ten times in the Pastoral Epistles, and only five times in the remainder of New Testament (1 Tim. 2:2; 3:16; 4:7, 8; 6:3, 5, 6, 11, 2 Tim. 3:5; Tit 1:1). The other occurrences are Acts 3:12; 2 Pet. 1:3, 6, 7; 3:11. The related verb *eusebeō* occurs in Acts 17:23 (translated 'worship') and 1 Tim. 5:4 ('shew piety'). The adverb *eusebōs*, translated 'godly' occurs in 2 Tim. 3:12 and Tit. 2:12.

[12] Towner, *Timothy*, 172. Towner's excursus on this subject (171–175) provides a useful discussion of the scholarship on *eusebeia* and its related terms.

And that, of course, is precisely the issue as far as these individuals are concerned. They have only a 'form' of godliness. The word 'form' can mean either 'appearance' or 'embodiment', but Paul uses it here in the former sense. These individuals have the external form of godliness – a superficial and empty religiosity. 'They liked the visible expressions, the ascetic practices, and the endless discussions of religious trivia, thinking themselves to be obviously righteous because they were obviously religious.'[13]

Despite their claims, however, they 'deny the power' of godliness. This denial has been delineated in verses 2–4. The selfish and savage tenor of these people's lives shows that they know nothing of the power that produces real godliness of living. That power is, ultimately, the power of God about which Paul has already spoken in this epistle (*cf.* 1:7, 8, 2:1). This power is provided by the indwelling Holy Spirit, and the lives of these people demonstrate that they know nothing of that reality.

Timothy's response must be to 'turn away' from these people, to 'have nothing to do with' them (NIV), to 'avoid' them (ESV, NET). This is another reason why society in general cannot be in view in these verses: our responsibility to preach the gospel is in no way diminished by the moral and spiritual devastation of society – rather the contrary. But false teachers of this ilk, those who masquerade as Christians while infiltrating error are to be avoided – Timothy must separate himself from them.

Verse 6 The language of verse 5 scarcely leaves scope for these individuals to be in fellowship in the assembly in Ephesus and that is borne out by their *modus operandi*, as

---

[13] Fee, *1 & 2 Timothy*, 270.

outlined in verses 6 and 7. Like wolves on the outskirts of a flock, they skulk on the periphery of the assembly. They 'creep' clandestinely into houses, worming themselves secretively into homes in order to take captives through deception. Their behaviour could hardly be less like that of Paul, who taught 'faithful men' publicly 'among 'many witnesses' (2:2). This point can hardly be overemphasised – the Scriptural pattern is for teaching to be given in the assembly and for all the assembly. Public teaching is accountable teaching, and we should always be cautious about teaching that is delivered in a covert or furtive manner.

It is significant that it is the home that comes under attack from these false teachers. The Pastoral Epistles have a great deal to say about the homes of believers and their importance for Christian testimony. In this epistle we are privileged to look into Timothy's childhood home (1:5, 3:15). Here, it is not necessarily the homes of believers that are in view – that is certainly not the main emphasis. But we do well to note the importance of our home life and the necessity to ensure that we defend our homes and our families against the depredations of error, always remembering that in the twenty-first century error need not creep in at the back door but can worm its way with great facility along the coils of our fibre connection.

The chosen quarry of these deceptive teachers is 'gullible women', literally 'little women', 'which was a scornful pejorative connoting "silly" or "foolish"'.[14] Paul is not making a sexist statement about women in general – only to the jaundiced eye of prejudice could Paul's wider remarks about women in this epistle or elsewhere be construed as disparaging. Rather, he is emphasising that these false teachers select the most vulnerable for

---

[14] Fee, *1 & 2 Timothy*, 272.

their prey. These women are further specified as being 'laden with sins'. These women have a sad history of unforgiven sin. Their problem is not just in the past, for they are presently 'led away with divers lusts'. 'Here the present passive participle refocuses on the present outworking of past sinfulness and depicts the effects as an inability to fight off harmful impulses.'[15]

Verse 7 These women are in a pitiable condition. And it is this condition, the burden of their consciences and the bondage of their will that make them so susceptible to the false teachers, whose teaching seems to offer the prospect of relief. But, like the inept physicians on whom the woman with the issue of blood had expended all her money, their spiritual treatment leaves their victims not better, but worse. These women are locked into an unending and unrewarding search for spiritual freedom, 'ever learning, and never able to come to the knowledge of the truth'. In these epistles, to 'come to the knowledge of the truth' is identified with salvation (*cf.* 1 Tim. 2:4), and it is salvation that these women need, to cleanse their guilty consciences and to give them the power of godliness that they so desperately need. The holy Scriptures (v. 15) could make them wise unto salvation, just as they did Timothy. But, because truth is precisely what these false teachers will not give them, and because the Scriptures are precisely what they do not teach they do nothing to help and everything to harm these vulnerable 'little women'.

Verse 8 From the beginning of this chapter Paul has painted a dark picture: the gloomy backdrop of ferocious times, peopled with the figures of corrupt and corrupting men, whose affections and appetites are

---

[15] Towner, *Timothy*, 562, 563.

distorted and who prey on the vulnerable. But he cannot bring this section to a close without allowing a glimmer of light to fall across the page. We already know that the progress of these wicked men will be brought to a halt, because we have seen their sort before. That is the main point of the reference to Jannes and Jambres, the Egyptian magicians who 'withstood Moses' (Exod. 7:11, 12, 22; 8:7). In just the same way as they opposed (*antestēsan*) Moses, so now these false teachers oppose (*anthistantai*) the truth. Their opposition, not just to Paul, but to the truth itself, reveals two aspects of their character. Firstly, they have corrupt minds. Their thinking has been utterly depraved. They lack the 'sound mind' of which Paul spoke in 1:7 of this epistle and the clear thinking which is highlighted repeatedly in Titus 2. The overthrow of their mental machinery is such that, rather than appreciating and appropriating truth, they repudiate and resist it. Moreover, they are 'reprobate [rejected or unfit] concerning the faith'. As is so often the case, there is some debate as to whether 'the faith' here is objective – paralleling the reference to truth – or subjective – i.e., the false teachers are rejected as to their own personal faith.[16] It is difficult to be dogmatic and unhelpful to make too absolute a dichotomy, but the context seems slightly to favour an objective sense. Held up against the standard of 'the faith', these teachers are revealed to be defective.

Verse 9 The real point of the historical comparison rings out in this verse. 'They shall proceed no further' says Paul. Just as the power of God made fools of the Egyptian magicians and revealed their empty pretension, so too will God stop the false teachers in their tracks and make

---

[16] The definite article '*the* faith' does appear here but contrary to popular belief that does not decide the issue one way or the other.

their folly known to all. There will be no hiding it – Paul's language emphasises the definitive clarity with which their folly will be revealed. Ferocious times will come, wicked men will worm and wheedle and withstand. But we already know how this story ends. Ultimately, truth will triumph.

Paul does not tell us how or when that will happen. However, the reference to Jannes and Jambres may provide some illumination. Their folly became manifest at the point when they had no ability to counterfeit genuine miracles, when their claims exceeded their power. In the same way, the ultimate fate of the false teachers is bound up with the powerlessness of the message they preach. Paul and Timothy and countless faithful men had proclaimed a message with innate power and again and again lives had been transformed as men and women were saved and came to the knowledge of the truth. The false teachers presented their own message as the panacea to the spiritual woes of their victims, but it changed nothing. Sooner or later, that would become clear and all the pretension, falsehood, and folly of the false teachers would be revealed. And time and again, in the 'last days' conditions that have extended from Timothy's lifetime to the present, that is precisely what has happened. Error has been constantly present, springing up in various forms but so often using precisely the tactics that Paul outlines in this chapter. It has made progress, gathering up adherents and reaping adulation for its apostles. But soon enough it runs out of road, and the false teachers have stood exposed as fools and frauds, just as Jannes and Jambres were, so long ago. And, though its progress often seems so glacially slow and although the forces arrayed against it seem at times irresistible, truth has endured and those who preach it, though often regarded as fools, have never truly been found so.

vv. 10–13 The faithfulness of the apostle

Verse 10 'But thou' – with this Paul turns decisively from error and its acolytes to deal with the truth and its followers: Paul himself and his faithful son Timothy. The false teachers will reappear briefly in verse 13 of this chapter and in verses 4 and 5 of the following chapter but, for the most part, the keynote of the epistle from this point forward is encouragement rather than warning. In contrast to the vices listed in verses 2 to 5 and their opposition to any sort of ordered relationship between individuals, Paul returns to a theme that has already featured in the epistle – his relationship with Timothy.

Timothy's intimate acquaintance with the details of Paul's life and teaching is summed up in the word 'fully known'. The KJV rendering here loses some of the force of the underlying word (*parakoloutheō*). Literally, this means 'so to follow one as to be always at his side' and, more metaphorically, 'to follow up a thing in mind so as to attain to the knowledge of it'.[17] Paul uses it to describe Timothy's intimate and immediate knowledge of the apostle's character and life. Timothy's grasp of these was not a mere academic apprehension. Nor did it arise from remote or casual observation. He knew Paul up close; he had walked with him and been a witness of his teaching, his service, and his suffering.

What Paul presents here is the New Testament ideal for teaching. We are consistently encouraged to judge a man's ministry by the life that it produces, and we can only know what that life is like if we are able to get close to those who teach us. Too often, we are apt to behave as

---

[17] Thayer, *Greek Lexicon*, s.v.

though the quality of teaching were in direct proportion to the distance that the servant has travelled to deliver it. Too often, it is the case that 'a prophet is not without honour, but in his own country' (Mk 6:4) – and too often we quote that text as though it offered some sort of justification for our preference for exotic speakers. It does not. Of course, local gift can be helpfully augmented by those who visit, and Barnabas' actions in bringing Paul to Antioch in Acts 11 are a useful demonstration of finding the right teacher to meet a specific need in a particular assembly. But we need to balance this with a deeper appreciation of those whose character allows them authoritatively to teach those who 'fully know' their manner of life.

It is striking and significant that, as Paul lists what Timothy knew about his life, he starts with 'my doctrine'. We might well have expected him to begin with 'manner of life'. After all, we have often been reminded that Ezra 'prepared his heart to seek the law of the LORD, and to do it, and to teach [it]' (Ezra 7:10) and that Luke describes the subject of his gospel as 'all ... that Jesus began both to do and teach' (Acts 1:1). And we will have been reminded of these things in order to make the point that doing comes before teaching and that, in the case of the Lord Jesus, the perfection of all that He did gave authority to all that He taught. Paul, however, is making a slightly different point here. That point has less to do with the issue of moral fitness to teach and more to do with the validation of doctrine by the life that it produces. Again and again throughout his epistles – and especially in the Pastorals – Paul stresses the relationship between doctrine and practice. False doctrine is always linked with immoral behaviour: the falseness of the teaching is revealed by the defectiveness of the life that it produces. Good doctrine, by contrast, the sound – or healthy – doctrine of which Paul so often speaks in the Pastorals, produces sound and healthy conduct. 'Ye shall know them by their fruits' (Mt. 7:16) is a principle that still applies and by beginning with his doctrine, Paul is emphasising the root from which all that was fruitful in his life originated. Well it is for us if our lives, too, are rooted in the teaching of Scripture and are marked by fruit that makes it clear that this is so.

It is precisely this link that Paul emphasises, for he moves from doctrine to 'manner of life', or conduct. The term takes us to the nitty-gritty of everyday life. Paul is thinking here, not so much of the big picture, but of the details of his daily life. Timothy's knowledge of Paul's life was in high resolution, and Paul knew that – and knew that there was nothing in his everyday existence that was inconsistent with the truth that he taught. All of us, but especially those of us that teach, should feel the challenge of his example, for too often there are too many false notes in our own life that do not harmonise with the truth we teach and profess to believe.

The routine of life matters. Paul's life, however, was not simply an accretion of events. It was marked by 'purpose'. Paul uses this word in 1:9 of God's purpose, and it conveys not just steadfastness and commitment, but the idea of a plan to be followed. There was nothing aimless about Paul's life; he always moved with the bigger picture clearly in mind. This was the man who pressed 'toward the mark for the prize of the high calling of God in Christ Jesus', who longed to 'apprehend that for which also [he was] apprehended of Christ Jesus' (Phil. 3:12, 14), whose 'ambition [was] to preach the gospel, not where Christ has already been named' (Rom. 15:20, ESV). Paul not only knew his purpose himself, but he was able to articulate it, and to communicate it to Timothy. Is it possible that, by contrast, we would struggle to articulate our sense of purpose to ourselves, never mind expressing it to someone else. The everyday matters, but there is always the danger that we can become so bogged down in the routine of living that we lose our sense of purpose, and begin live as though we had no goal beyond surviving until the weekend. May God give us help to avoid aimless, directionless lives and to live with purpose.

Living a life with purpose is hard. To articulate, even if only to ourselves, a purpose is to raise the possibility that we will fail to achieve it. Faced with the challenge, it is all too easy to just not try. But, though the difficulties are real enough, the answer is not to avoid them but to overcome them. And so, Paul moves next to the only thing that could adequately fortify him – or any of us – for the challenge: his faith in God. Although 'faithful' can also mean loyal or dependable, the context here makes it more likely that Paul is stressing the reality of his reliance upon God – not so much his faithfulness to God, as his faith in God. Throughout this epistle, Paul has been urging Timothy to depend on God, and he has modelled that dependence in his own life.

Paul moves from the vertical to the horizontal axis of relationship with the next characteristic he highlights. 'Longsuffering' or patience is repeatedly identified in the New Testament not just as a feature that should mark the believer, but as a characteristic of God Himself. In 4:2, Paul identifies it as an essential element of the ministry of the 'man of God'. In one way or another, Paul had had a fair bit of provocation from those he ministered to. But, in response to it, he had demonstrated the same sort of patience that marked the God that he served.

Patience is important, but an attitude to others comprised only of putting up with them would be a rather grim affair. 'Charity', or love moves beyond the passive to the active, beyond endurance to endeavour, to the sacrificial service of others. Paul, as Saul, had been a notable hater – his hatred of Christ and His people had spurred him to zealous acts of persecution. But on the Damascus road all that had changed, and Paul's love became even more ardent than his hatred had been. Even though he, at times, had to lament 'the more abundantly I love you, the less I be loved' (2 Cor. 12:15), he went on loving just the same. Timothy had known that love himself and had seen it displayed to others. He fully knew its depth, its sincerity, and the sacrifice it involved.

'Patience' – the final word of this verse serves as the coda to the catalogue of suffering that follows in verse 11. 'Long suffering' is patience with people, 'patience' (better, perhaps, 'endurance') is patience with circumstances and events, a willingness to withstand 'even the greatest trials and sufferings'.[18] In fact, it is something even more than that, for this endurance is not a grim plugging alone, with hunched shoulders and gritted teeth. Rather it is 'cheerful (or hopeful) endurance'.[19] Paul had had much to endure – the next verse leaves us in no doubt of that. But he had endured, and Timothy, who knew so much about him, could witness to it.

Verse 11 In verse 10, Paul reminded Timothy of his intimate and immediate knowledge of the apostle's 'doctrine, manner of life, purpose, faith, longsuffering, charity, patience'. It is worthy of note that each of these terms is in the singular – a fact that emphasises the consistency of the apostle's life. He reminded Timothy

---

[18] Thayer, *Greek Lexicon, s.v.*
[19] Strongs, *s.v.*

of his teaching and of the character that that teaching had produced in his life, in its everyday details as well as its overarching purpose, in his relationship with God and with his fellow men. Verse 10 concludes with Paul's patience – his cheerful and hopeful endurance of difficult circumstances. In verse 11 he outlines the context in which that endurance – and the other facets of his character – had been displayed. The change to the plural – 'persecutions, afflictions' – stresses the reality and the multiplicity of these experiences. Persecutions and afflictions were nothing exceptional in Paul's life.

The two terms overlap in meaning. 'Persecutions' describes those sufferings that he endured because of his proclamation of the gospel, while 'afflictions' is an embracive term for sufferings in general. Paul highlights three places where he had suffered affliction: Antioch, Iconium, and Lystra. There were, of course, no shortage of places that he could have mentioned, and we might well have expected him to refer to the sufferings that he was enduring even as he wrote. But Paul chooses instead to go right back almost to the beginning of his first missionary journey, right back, in fact, before Timothy had even joined him. In Antioch (Acts 13:14–52), Iconium (Acts 14:1–5), and Lystra (Acts 14:6–19), Jewish opposition to the preaching of the gospel had stirred up persecution, which reached its climax in Lystra, where Paul was stoned and left for dead (Acts 14:19).

Paul's reference back to the early days of his Christian service is not incidental. Rather, it serves two purposes. Firstly, it stresses the constancy of opposition. Timothy could not suppose that Paul's sufferings were a recent phenomenon or some sort of anomaly in Paul's experience. Right from the beginning, Paul had known persecution. Secondly, 'part of the appeal to loyalty in this letter is to remind Timothy of his origins. It is Paul's way of saying: "Look, you were there in Lystra when I was stoned. You recall that such sufferings were visible to you from the time you began your Christian walk. So don't bail out now in the midst of this present – and coming – distress."'[20]

These reasons account for Paul's mention of these specific instances of suffering, but his mention of sufferings also serves two wider purposes. In connection with the preceding verse, it reminds Timothy of the context in which the characteristics mentioned in verse 10 had been displayed. Paul's patience, love, and endurance had not just been fair weather flowers that had withered at the first gust of a contrary wind. Rather, his character had been displayed – and Timothy had come to know it – in circumstances of extreme adversity. Reflecting on those circumstances, Paul exclaims 'what persecutions I endured!'[21]

Paul's account of his sufferings also sets up two broader points that he wants to make – for faithful believers, suffering is inevitable, but deliverance is sure. It is in keeping with his purpose of encouragement that he begins with deliverance. Paul endured the persecutions – he held out beneath them – but his deliverance came ultimately, not from his own tenacity and endurance, but from Divine deliverance. 'Out of them all the Lord delivered me'. The language here echoes that of Psalm 34:17 and 19 ('The righteous cry, and the LORD heareth, and delivereth them out of all their troubles'; 'Many are the afflictions of the righteous: but

---

[20] Fee, *1 & 2 Timothy*, 277
[21] A number of translations supply the exclamation point, making it explicit that this is an exclamation wrung from Paul by his recollection of the sufferings that he endured. This is altogether more persuasive than the NIV rendering ('persecutions, sufferings—what kinds of things happened to me in Antioch, Iconium and Lystra, the persecutions I endured'), which reduces the clause to mere repetition.

the LORD delivereth him out of them all').²² This echo underlines Divine sovereignty in the deliverance of the apostle – it is the Lord Who rescues him, and Who delivers him comprehensively – 'out of them *all*', (*cf.* 4:18). It also aligns the apostle's sufferings with those of the righteous identified by the psalmist and lays the ground for his second point – sufferings like these are inevitable for those who 'will live godly'.

Verse 12 Paul's turn from his own experience to highlight a general principle is emphatic. Paul's sufferings were prodigious, but they were also unexceptionable. Contrary to what some commentators have suggested, neither Paul nor a later imitator are trying to 'canonise' the apostle by suggesting that there was something unique in his sufferings. Paul is making precisely the opposite point – he is a pattern for Timothy and for 'all' in his sufferings as well as in his life, for it is a general principle that 'all who desire to live a godly life in Christ Jesus will be persecuted' (ESV). We have noted in our discussion of verse 5 of this chapter that the concept of 'godliness' is an important distinctive of the Pastoral Epistles. Here, Christians are described as those 'who desire to live a godly life in Christ Jesus'. The emphasis on the volition is striking – Christians are resolved to live a godly life. That resolve alone is sufficient to qualify believers for persecution, and the corollary of a desire to live godly is the resolve to suffer persecution. This is a challenging phrase. We would all play lip service to the importance of living a godly life, but can it really be said of us that we are resolved to do so? And, in a world where any illusions that we might have about being able to escape reproach and avoid persecution are fast being whittled away, do we have the

---

²² Towner, *Timothy*, 575.

determination to live as those who know God – and accept the consequences that a godless society deems appropriate. But, as we feel the challenge of the verse let us notice, too, the resource to which it points us – believers are those who live 'in Christ Jesus' and our strength to endure, as well as our assurance of ultimate deliverance, comes from Him.

Verse 13 Paul reemphasises the Christian's hope of deliverance by drawing a further contrast with the false teachers: 'But evil men and seducers shall wax worse and worse, deceiving, and being deceived'. The twofold description of these men moves from the general 'evil men' to the more specific 'seducers' or imposters. 'The evil aspect of their character is described in vv. 2–5, whilst the seductive aspect is outlined in vv. 6–9.'[23] 'Seducers' is a 'rare term [which] ranges in meaning from the technical sense of a "sorcerer" (who deceives by practicing magic and witchcraft) to the broader sense of "deceiver, cheat, charlatan".'[24] The technical sense resonates with Paul's earlier mention of Jannes and Jambres, but in both instances, Paul is making a broader point about those who engage in deception – 'deceiving, and being deceived'. Here, as in 2:16, Paul uses the language of progress and development ironically – the false teachers are making progress, but in the wrong direction – they are going 'from bad to worse' (*ESV, NIV, NET*).

A point that deserves consideration is whether the apostle here is thinking of this progression in evil personally or dispensationally. The verse has often been read as a statement by the apostle that, as the present dispensation progresses, so evil men and seducers will

---

[23] Baker, *II Timothy*, 370.
[24] Towner, *Timothy*, 578.

become worse – more evil, more active, and more successful in deceiving their victims. This reading is informed by the idea that the 'perilous times' and 'last days' of verse 1 describe the unfolding stages of the dispensation. However, as we have seen, it is by no means certain that this is the case, and even if we do understand verse 1 in this way, it is difficult satisfactorily to account for a shift from the personal to the dispensational in these verses.

Given the point that the apostle is making and the flow of his argument, it seems altogether more likely that he is speaking of the false teachers as individuals. These men have embarked on a downward trajectory from which they cannot escape – they progress to the worse, deceiving others and being deceived themselves. Unless they repent of their error there can be no deliverance for them, and no genuine progress.[25] Though they may avoid persecution and seem, outwardly and temporarily to enjoy success, they are neither to be envied nor emulated.

In these verses, Paul has presented himself as a pattern for believers more generally. His doctrine and the character of the life that it produced should be reproduced in Timothy's life and in the life of other believers. But to follow Paul's doctrine and to imitate Paul's life is to share, too, in Paul's sufferings. But even when we do so, the fact that we are 'in Christ Jesus' and destined for glory and guaranteed ultimate deliverance means that our lot is happier than that of any evil imposter.

---

[25] It is, of course, not impossible for both the personal and the dispensational to be in view in these verses. Even if this is the case, the flow of argument demands that Paul's focus is on the personal.

vv. 14–17   The Fulness of the Scriptures

Verse 14 The emphatic second person pronoun at the beginning of this verse turns our attention away from the 'evil men and seducers' of verse 13 and back onto Timothy's individual responsibility.[26] We have already noted that this is characteristic of this epistle. Although Paul repeatedly speaks about the wider background to Timothy's ministry, he never allows him to forget that what is really important is not the darkness and difficulty that surrounds him, but his own responsibility to be God's man in the circumstances and context in which he finds himself. We often find a contemplation of the hostile world that we live in a distraction and an occasion for despair. Sometimes we use our context as an excuse for our fruitlessness and faithlessness. For Paul, by contrast, the surrounding gloom serves as a spur to increased steadfastness in the service of God. In contrast to the downward spiral of evil men and seducers waxing 'worse and worse', Timothy is to continue – better, to abide or to dwell – in the truth that he has received.

Before examining in detail what Paul has to say about what Timothy is to abide in, it is worth taking a step back in order to grasp the overall flow of Paul's argument in this paragraph. Paul reminds Timothy of the two great bodies of truth that he has received. The first is described as 'the things which thou hast learned and hast been assured of'. These 'things' are the teachings of the apostle, received from Paul himself, validated by the character of his life and the reality of his sufferings, and fully known by Timothy (v. 10). [27] The second, outlined

---

[26] The word order in the Greek is 'You however, continue...'.
[27] There is some disagreement in the manuscripts as to whether 'whom' is singular or plural. If singular it refers to Paul alone. If the plural is to be preferred, the expression includes others who have taught Timothy the

in verse 15, is the 'sacred writings' (*hiera grammata*), which Timothy knew from his childhood. The term that Paul uses to describe these 'sacred writings' is found only here in the New Testament but is used elsewhere as a technical designation for all or part of the Hebrew Bible, our Old Testament.[28]

Paul then does a remarkable thing. With one hand, he takes the holy writings, the revered Jewish Scriptures, God's Word to his ancient people; with the other he takes the apostolic teachings that Timothy had received. Then he brings them together under a single – and singular – description: *graphe*, 'Scripture'. This word is frequently used in the New Testament to describe the Old Testament Scriptures in part or in whole. Significantly, Peter also uses it to describe the epistles of Paul (2 Pet. 3:16), and in 1 Timothy 5:18 Paul applies it to a quotation from Luke's gospel. Here, Paul is using it in a sense that subsumes these usages – as a term to describe the whole Bible – Old Testament and New. The truth of God communicated by the apostle is placed on an equal footing with Old Testament revelation (just as it is in 2 Pet. 3:2).[29] The crucial point is clear: whether the Old Testament or the New, all

---

apostolic doctrine and may also include Lois and Eunice – who are certainly in view in the following verse. See Stott, *2 Timothy*, 98–99 for a convincing argument that only Paul is in view.

[28] Towner, *Timothy*, 582–3.

[29] This argument differs from the more usual suggestion that 'all Scripture' refers in context to the Old Testament (but see John Stott, *2 Timothy*, 101), but avoids the necessity to explain why Paul uses two different words for the same thing (*grammata*, v. 15, *graphe*, v. 16) (see also the discussion in Towner, *Timothy*, 582–587). The argument assumes that Timothy knew Paul's teaching in its written form. This is likely, not least because Paul's reference to the 'parchments' that Timothy is to bring to him (2 Tim. 4:13) used a Latin loanword that (while it occurs only here in Scripture) was used to describe the codex, the rudimentary books which early Christians overwhelmingly preferred for the transmission of Scripture. See the discussion at pp. 194, 195 below.

Scripture is given by inspiration of God. And precisely because all Scripture is God-breathed, it is profitable for the man of God and has the capacity to equip him for every need that he will face.

With that outline of Paul's argument in our minds, we can turn again to the detail of verse 14 and notice that two terms describe Timothy's relationship with the truth that he has been taught by the apostle – he has 'learned' it and 'been assured of' it. 'Learned' is the same word as that used of the foolish women in verse 6, but, while they were locked in a loop of futile learning, Timothy's education has led to assurance, to wisdom, and ultimately to his complete equipment for 'all good works'. The verb rendered 'been assured of' can be interpreted in two ways. It can mean 'have become convinced of' (so, NIV) or 'been faithful to'.[30] Either sense would fit the context here, but on balance, while it is true that the latter reading 'corresponds more closely to the contrast developing between Timothy's commitment to the faith and the heretical rejection of it',[31] the former seems to fit better with the basis that Paul gives for Timothy's confidence in what he has learned. Timothy has not merely acquired an academic knowledge of the truth, nor has he simply adopted 'traditionalism or the status quo'.[32] Rather, he has embraced the truth with conviction – he is entirely convinced of its reliability. A mere intellectual acquiescence to Scripture is not sufficient – if we are to continue in the things we have learned – and we must – then we must also be convinced and convicted of their truth. Timothy had that assurance, and he had a basis for

---

[30] Towner, *Timothy*, 580.
[31] Towner, *Timothy*, 581.
[32] Knight III, *The Pastoral Epistles*, New International Greek Testament Commentary (Grand Rapids, MI: Eerdmans, 1992), 442.

it: 'knowing of whom thou hast learned them'. This echoes verse 10, where Paul stressed Timothy's intimate knowledge of his life. Here, too, Paul is insistent on the importance of knowing those who teach us, of being able to observe godly lives that lend credibility to the doctrine taught.

Verse 15 The importance of this is further underscored as the apostle reminds Timothy of his upbringing. Already in this epistle, we have had a glimpse into Timothy's childhood home (1:5) and here, as there, Paul's purpose is to remind Timothy of his roots. In contrast to all the churn and upheaval of the false teachers and their teaching, Timothy can look back to his 'infancy' (NIV, NET) and the Scriptures that he learned at his mother's – and his grandmother's – knee. In contrast to teaching that was powerless (v. 5) and unable to produce 'the knowledge of the truth', the Scriptures have power 'to make wise unto salvation' (*cf.* Ps. 19:7). There is in this verse a mandate for the vital work of mothers in teaching the Scriptures to their children in the home. Timothy never outgrew that instruction, for it was not only able to make him wise unto salvation, in the initial sense of bringing him to faith in Christ, but, as the present tense indicates, it continued to do so. And the salvation that he learned about is 'through faith which is in Christ Jesus'. That is to say, it is the salvation proclaimed in the gospel that Paul preached, for there is no disconnect between Old Testament and New Testament revelation, and the message that Paul preached was altogether consistent with the Scriptures that had filled Timothy's childhood (*cf.* Acts 26:22, 23). 'False teaching cannot deliver the promise of salvation. Paul's gospel, on the other hand, grounded as it is in the truth of Christ's death and resurrection, completes the ancient revelation in a way that augments and releases its power to save.'[33]

Timothy was to continue. Even when others departed from the truth, lurching outwards and downwards into deception and darkness, he was to stand fast. That stand was not born of a stubborn intransigence or of a reactionary love of tradition. It came rather from the depth of Timothy's conviction about the truth of Divine revelation, a conviction that took its power from the character of those who had taught him. For those of us who teach God's people, the lesson is both solemn and salutary – character matters. And for all of us, Timothy's faithfulness is an example and an exhortation. May we, like him, have a deep conviction about the truth of God's Word so that we, in days as dark as his, may continue in the things that we have learned.

Verse 16 In this verse, Paul moves beyond the human conduit of the teaching that Timothy had received and any argument from antiquity to identify the real source of the Scriptures' reliability and power. All Scripture, whether the Hebrew Bible of Timothy's youth or the revelation recorded in the writings of the apostle 'is given by inspiration of God'. It would be difficult to overstate the importance of this verse or the significance of its statement that 'all Scripture is given by inspiration of God'. It is incumbent upon us, therefore, to consider this statement in some detail.

There are two questions that arise from the grammar of this expression: 1. Should the Greek adjective *pasa* be rendered 'all' (as it is in the KJV and most other translations) or as 'every' (as in the ASV and NET)? 2. Should *theopneustos* ('God-breathed', rendered 'given by inspiration of God' in the KJV) be understood 'as an

---

[33] Towner, *Timothy*, 584.

attributive adjective modifying *graphē* ("every [all] God-breathed Scripture is useful...") or as a predicate adjective ... ("every [all] Scripture is inspired and useful...").[34] The different permutations of these options give us four possible ways of understanding this clause:

> A1: All Scripture is God-breathed and profitable ...
> A2: Every Scripture is God-breathed and profitable ...
> B1: All God-breathed Scripture is profitable ...
> B2: Every God-breathed Scripture is profitable ...

What is immediately apparent is that relatively little hinges on the choice between 'all' and 'every'.[35] There is undoubtedly a difference in nuance between the two – to say 'I got my hairs cut' is not quite the same thing as saying 'I got my hair cut' – but the difference is slight. 'Every Scripture' would tend to emphasise the value of each component of Scripture, while 'all Scripture' emphasises Scripture as a totality. If, as we have suggested, Paul is speaking here of the gathering together of Old and New Testament Scripture then 'all' seems the best choice in context, and it is certainly the option that has recommended itself (for a range of reasons) to the sizable majority of translators.

The second decision is, perhaps, more consequential. If Paul is saying that all (or every) God-breathed Scripture is useful, he seems to allow for the possibility that there are some Scriptures that are not God-

---

[34] Towner, *Timothy*, 585
[35] From a technical perspective, the debate hinges on whether 'Scripture' is a collective noun or one which refers to items individually. 'Scripture' can be either, though it must be acknowledged that Paul's normal usage tends to favour the latter (though see Galatians 3:22 and, outside of Paul's writings, 2 Peter 3:16). Ultimately, grammar alone is inconclusive and our final decision must be based on the context.

breathed. This understanding is highly unlikely on contextual and grammatical grounds. Grammatically, it 'violates the parallelism of the two adjectives in the sentence, and the arrangement of words makes clear that both should be taken as predicate adjectives: "every scripture is inspired...and useful."'[36] The context supports this: for Paul to suggest to Timothy that his faith was to rest only on some special portions of the Scriptures would run counter to the whole emphasis of this section and of the epistle as a whole. That idea was favoured by later heretics and still is by some of their modern progeny, but it is foreign to the thinking of the Apostle Paul and should be equally foreign to ours. All Scripture, Paul is saying, is God-breathed and profitable.

Theopneustos is a term that is not found elsewhere in the New Testament, and it has been suggested that Paul is coining a new word to describe what we usually speak of as the inspiration of Scripture.[37] The term 'inspiration', which came into English from Latin has never been a particularly accurate reflection of what Paul is saying in this verse, and it has become less so as the term has increasingly acquired a non-theological meaning. When we describe the creative process, we speak, in common parlance, of a poet or a painter as being inspired, moved by a creative impulse to produce a poem or a painting. By contrast, it is not strictly accurate to speak of the human authors of Scripture as 'inspired writers'. While it is true that Peter tells us that 'holy men of God spake as they were moved by the Holy Ghost', Paul is speaking here of inspired words, and not inspired writers. More accurately, he is speaking of

---

[36] *New English Translation*, translator's note to 2 Timothy 3:16.
[37] Marshall, *Pastoral Epistles*, 794. See B.B. Warfield, *The Inspiration and Authority of the Bible*, (London: Marshall, Morgan, and Scott Ltd, 1951), 245–96 for an extensive discussion of the term.

words that have been breathed out by God. The imagery vividly conveys not just the origin of the words but their power and energy as well. The cliché is no less remarkable and no less true for its familiarity – the Scriptures are indeed warm with the breath of God. God's Word is living and powerful. And it is on the power and the profit of Scripture that Paul focuses; its indispensable importance for the 'man of God'.

Scripture 'is profitable for doctrine, for reproof, for correction, for instruction in righteousness'. A number of points about this list are worth noticing. Firstly, it is significant that it combines doctrine and practice. 'Teaching' is followed by 'reproof', a word that has the idea of pointing out someone's sinful behaviour. 'Correction', again, focuses on practice – it moves beyond rebuke to recovery and the inculcation of correct behaviour. The list concludes with 'instruction in righteousness', where 'instruction' translates a word that means education or training. This blending of doctrine and practice would have come as no surprise to Timothy, though it might, perhaps, to some of us. The interplay of teaching and the behaviour that it produces is emphasised by the structure of the sentence – the chiastic structure doctrine-practice-practice-doctrine indicates that proper Christian conduct is wrapped up in correct doctrine.

Secondly, we should note that the list balances positive and negative. 'Teaching' is a positive action, the communication of doctrine. 'Reproof', the identification and censure of sinful behaviour, is negative (though it should always be undertaken with a positive aim). Similarly, 'correction', while positive in its aim, implies a context where there is something to be corrected. 'Instruction in righteousness' has no such negative connotation. God's Word has power both for cultivation of what is good and wholesome, or the censure of what is bad and damaging. All of us, at various times, will require both instruction and correction from Scripture and the fact that it is God-breathed guarantees its ability to speak to the circumstances of our lives, in all their variety.

Thirdly, we should notice that the ability of Scripture as outlined in this verse aligns closely with Timothy's responsibility to 'preach the word ... reprove, rebuke, exhort with all longsuffering and doctrine' (4:2). A fuller treatment of that verse will have to wait until we get to it but the connection is important, for it exemplifies the way in which the Scriptures are able to 'throughly furnish' the man of God.

The fact that Scripture is God-breathed means that it is sufficient to make the man of God complete and completely equipped for every good work. The way that Paul piles up the language here is striking – he emphasises the ability of Scripture to fully furnish the man of God for every circumstance and challenge that he will face. What is less clear is how we are to understand the expression 'man of God'. Clearly it applied to Timothy, but does it apply to all believers (or all male believers) and if so, does it apply in the same way as it did to Timothy? Translators have expanded and interpreted the expression in a variety of ways: 'servant of God' (*NIV*), 'man [or woman] of God' (*NASB*), 'the person dedicated to God' (*NET*). These translations are motivated by a desire to stress that Scripture is sufficient for every believer in his or her service for God. That, of course, is true, but contextually, Paul has something more specific in mind. In the Old Testament, the expression 'man of God' 'is applied (over thirty times) exclusively to Moses and the prophets who follow in his footsteps.'[38] Already in this chapter (vv. 8, 9) Paul has established a parallel between his and Timothy's ministry and that of Moses. While it is true that every believer should desire to be 'a servant of God' and 'a person dedicated to God' and while it is true that those who do dedicate themselves to God and His service will find every resource that they need in the pages of Scripture, 'man of God' is a term that is used in a special way of Timothy and of those males who continue his work of teaching the truth of God and withstanding the error of false teachers.

---

[38] Towner, *Timothy*, 593.

Chapter Four

4:1–8 The Alertness of the Man of God

v. 1 The Solemnity of the Charge

IT WOULD BE DIFFICULT TO overstate the solemnity of the word with which this chapter opens. The word 'charge' and the calling to witness of 'God and of Christ Jesus, who is to judge the living and the dead, and ... His appearing and his kingdom' (ESV) lend tremendous weight to Paul's instructions to Timothy. This is not the first time that he has received a charge like this. In 1 Timothy 5:21, Paul used similar language: 'I charge thee before God, and the Lord Jesus Christ, and the elect angels, that thou observe these things'.[1] In both epistles, the final charge is designed to bring home to Timothy the implications that Paul's teaching has for him personally. The personal nature of the charge brings to bear not just the relationship that existed between Timothy and Paul but the full force of Paul's apostolic authority.

Above and beyond this authority, however, is the authority of Divine Persons. Timothy is responsible, not just to Paul, but to 'God and Christ Jesus'. Paul is not just stressing the fact that Timothy's service is carried out from day to day under Divine scrutiny – though that is true – but the reality that the day is coming when Timothy's service will be evaluated and reward will be

---

[1] The word is also used in 2:14 of this epistle, where Timothy is instructed to charge the believers 'that they strive not about words to no profit'. Paul gives a similar charge, using a different verb, in 1 Timothy 6:13.

apportioned. Paul states the general principle of Christ's role as judge – He is the One who is about to judge the living and the dead. For Timothy, as for all believers in this dispensation, that judgement will take place at the *bema*, the Judgement Seat of Christ, and its purpose will be to apportion reward for service.[2] That this is the judgement specifically in view in this passage is confirmed by the following expression: 'and by his appearing and his kingdom' (ESV). This rendering is preferable to the KJV's 'at his appearing and his kingdom'. Although 'the relationship of this phrase to the preceding statement about judging the living and the dead is somewhat awkward in English',[3] the expression is best understand not as giving the time of the judgement, but as relating back to the charge – it is given 'in view of His appearing and His kingdom' (NIV). 'Appearing' (*epiphaneia*) is a distinctive word in the Pastoral epistles. In 2 Timothy 1:10, it is used of the first appearance of the Lord Jesus Christ, but elsewhere it looks forwards to His manifestation in glory (1 Tim. 6:14; 2 Tim. 4:1, 8; Tit. 2:13).[4] As the grammar here emphasises, there is a very close connection between Christ's appearing and the establishment of His kingdom.[5] The relevance of these events to the charge is important: it is at Christ's appearing and kingdom that the faithfulness with which Timothy has carried out this charge will be

---

[2] *Cf.* Romans 14:10, 2 Corinthians 5:10. See, for a more complete discussion of the Judgement Seat, Mark Sweetnam, *To the Day of Eternity: Future Events in Bible Prophecy*, (Lisburn: Scripture Teaching Library, 2014), 45–49.

[3] Towner, *Timothy*, 601, but *cf.* Stott, *2 Timothy*, 596, 597.

[4] The word is used elsewhere in the NT only in 2 Thessalonians 2:8, where it is translated as 'the brightness [of His coming]'.

[5] The expression could be rendered 'His appearing through [or in] His kingdom', see the discussion in Jerome D. Quinn and William C. Wacker, *The First and Second Letters to Timothy: A New Translation with Notes and Commentary*, (Grand Rapids, MI: Eerdmans 2000), 773.

manifest. The language echoes the emphasis on reward and reign that we have already seen in chapter 2.

v. 2 The Scope of the Charge

The content of Paul's charge to Timothy is outlined in a series of five imperatives. We should probably understand the last four as expanding the initial command to 'preach the Word': it is certainly the case that the instruction to 'preach the Word 'plays a dominant role';[6] the four imperatives that follow emphasise the 'how' of Timothy's preaching. But Paul first stresses the 'what' – Timothy is to 'preach the Word'. This is the message described as 'the Word of God' in 2:9 and 'the Word of truth' in 2:15. In the context of the verses at the end of the previous chapter, it seems artificial and unnecessary to make a distinction between 'the Pauline gospel' and Scripture as a whole – Timothy is to preach the Scriptures. To preach means to announce as a herald. Preaching is God's chosen method for the communication of Divine truth in this dispensation (Tit. 1:3). It involves the public announcement of truth by a single, authoritative voice. Although it is increasingly unfashionable in a society dominated by the visual and accustomed to consuming information in ever shorter bursts, preaching is not something that we can abandon or replace with another form of communication. We are responsible, as Timothy was, to 'preach the Word'.

In his responsibility to preach, Timothy is to 'be instant in season, out of season'. The verb rendered 'be instant' in the KJV has at its root the idea of standing near, and conveys the sense of proximity in place or time or readiness for opportunity. In this context, it can convey the idea of preparedness (NIV, ESV, etc.) or of

---

[6] Knight III, *Pastoral Epistles*, 453.

persistence (*HCSB*, *NRSV*). In either case, it emphasises Timothy's responsibility to be prepared at any moment and in all circumstances to preach. 'In season, out of season' means whether it is convenient or inconvenient. There is some debate as to whether this means when it is convenient for Timothy or for his hearers, but it seems clear that Paul intends the latter. The terms were used in the context of philosophical debates 'where the need to discern the appropriate time to speak so as to be most persuasive to a particular audience was stressed'.[7] This resonates with the words of verse 3: 'the time will come when they will not endure sound doctrine'. This expression conveys something of the urgency of Paul's charge, but there is no suggestion that Timothy is to stop preaching when that time comes – whether his audience finds it convenient or not, whether they are in an ideal state or not, whether they are thirsty for truth or eager for error, Timothy is to keep on preaching.

Timothy is to preach regardless of whether his audience is prepared to listen or not. But this does not mean that he can preach regardless of his listeners' needs. Rather, as the next three imperatives indicate, his preaching must address the need and condition of his hearers. This will not always be a very appealing task, for Timothy's task as a preacher will require him to 'reprove' his listeners, 'to call [them] to account, show one his fault'.[8] This is a necessary step in preaching the gospel to unbelievers. For believers, too, especially those who have been led astray by the lure of false teaching, being brought to an awareness and acknowledgement of sin is essential. Those who are involved in sin must not only be convicted, they must also be 'rebuked': 'openly

---

[7] Towner, *Timothy*, 107.
[8] Thayer, *Greek Lexicon*, s.v.

challenged with error or sin'.[9] Happily, there is a positive side to preaching, for Timothy is also to 'exhort', to encourage and comfort believers, to urge them on to increased spiritual maturity. This is where preaching's centre of gravity really lies, and its importance is emphasised by the addition of a phrase explaining how this exhorting is to be done: 'with all longsuffering and doctrine'. That patience will be needed for teaching will only come as a surprise to someone who has never done it. Even encouraging words of exhortation may not produce immediate results – Timothy must be prepared to try and try and try again, and not to give up simply because his preaching appears not to have an immediate impact. Exhortation must also be with 'doctrine', or teaching. The exhortation that Paul has in mind here is not the sort of motivational pep talk that we sometimes dignify with the name. Rather, it has its roots in 'the Word' and encourages the saints by instructing them in the Scriptures.

This charge embraces a variegated range of responsibility, gathered under that activity of preaching, to be sure, but requiring quite a degree of versatility and flexibility on Timothy's part. Well it is, then, that he had access to a resource which (he has been told just sentences ago) is able to equip the man of God fully 'unto all good works' (2 Tim. 3:17). The Scriptures that are profitable for 'doctrine, for reproof, for correction, for instruction in righteousness' are precisely what Timothy needs if he is to 'preach the word; be instant in season, out of season; reprove, rebuke, exhort with all longsuffering and doctrine'.

Paul's charge is weighty, and we need to feel its weight just as Timothy did, for the priorities of Timothy's preaching must be ours too. Timothy was to preach 'the

---

[9] Towner, *Timothy*, 601.

Word'. Not psychology, not politics, not systematic theology, certainly not his own imagination or personality, but 'the Word'. Timothy had no business preaching anything else and neither have we. Timothy was to be ready to preach and to go on preaching, whether his audience was receptive or not. His mission was too important to be subject to his audience's appetite. He was to give them what they needed, even if and even when they didn't desire or appreciate it. He was not to shirk even such unpleasant responsibilities as bringing people face-to-face with their sin and calling for their repentance. He could not tailor his teaching to the whims of audience appreciation and tempting though it often is, no more can we if we are faithfully to discharge in our own generation the compelling command to 'preach the Word'.

vv. 3–5 The Season of the Charge

Verse 3 Verses 1 and 2 of this chapter outline a solemn and urgent charge. With a consciousness of Christ as Judge and an appreciation of a coming day of manifestation and reward, Timothy was to 'preach the Word', with diligence and discernment, when his audience was receptive, and when it was not. As the 'for' that opens verse 3 indicates, verses 3 and 4 give the reason for the urgency and the seriousness of the charge. Timothy's discharge of his responsibility must be governed by the fact that 'the time will come when they will not endure sound doctrine'. Significantly, the word translated 'time' is *kairos*, which echoes the words for 'in season' (*eukairōs*) and 'out of season' (*akairōs*). The thought is not so much that Timothy must preach assiduously now, because the time is coming when that preaching will find no audience. Rather, Paul's primary message is that, even when this time comes, Timothy must still, undeterred, 'preach the Word'.

Paul does not identify when this time will arrive, and commentators have offered different possibilities. Towner suggests that Paul is speaking about present contemporary conditions, arguing that 'the effect of the future ... is to create the sense of fulfilment of eschatological realities'.[10] Similarly, Mounce argues that 'the prophecy is stated as a future reality but a future that has now been realised in Timothy's present.'[11] Knight, by contrast, argues that Paul is speaking about future events so that Timothy is 'forewarned that such a situation will arise'.[12] On balance, the fact that the focus of this verse is not on false teachers specifically but, more generally, on those to whom their teaching appeals seems to indicate a progression beyond what Paul has spoken about at the beginning of chapter 3 and suggests that he is speaking about a situation that is imminent, rather than immediate.

In the not very distant future, Paul anticipates, there will come time when error will no longer be contained but will have infected many – perhaps even the majority of – professing believers. Paul tells us four things about the attitudes and action of these people, and there appears to be a progression – or, rather, a decline – between one stage and the next.

The first step on this downward road is an unwillingness to 'endure sound doctrine'. Sound, or healthful, doctrine is one of the key motifs of the Pastoral Epistles. Throughout these epistles it is presented as a vital requisite for a robust spiritual life and it stands in opposition to the diseased and diseasing

---

[10] Towner, 603, see also Marshall, *Pastoral Epistles*, 801–802.
[11] Mounce, *Pastoral Epistles*, 574.
[12] Knight III, *Pastoral Epistles*, 455.

teaching of the false teachers. But where there should be an appetite, instead there is an aversion. These individuals will, literally, 'not put up with' sound doctrine – their reaction 'is described in terms of boredom, apathy, or annoyance'.[13] Searchingly, the downward path of these people begins very quietly, almost, perhaps, imperceptibly, with an attitude of impatience with the teaching of sound doctrine. We should all take heed of this – our attitude to the teaching of the Word of God is an important barometer of our spiritual health: to dismiss that teaching as boring, irrelevant, or unnecessary is an alarming indication of a possible spiritual pathology.

Turning from sound doctrine leaves a vacuum that must be filled and when truth no longer appeals, the only option is to fill the space with error. This is precisely what these people do – 'after their own lusts shall they heap to themselves teachers, having itching ears'. These people are led, not by a desire for what is healthy and wholesome, but by their own depraved desires. Their choice of teachers is determined by those desires – a word that is always used in a negative sense in the Pastoral Epistles. Paul's language here verges upon mockery as he imagines these people gathering a great stockpile of false teachers: 'rather than hearing one correct teacher, they build a wall of teachers as if the sheer number of teachers will make them right'.[14] And these teachers say nothing to challenge their listeners. 'Having itching ears' is figurative language that may imagine the false teachers 'scratching the itch' for these people or that may describe their teaching as mere ear-tickling. In either case, the point being made is the same: there is no substance to this teaching, and no edge, it is

---

[13] Towner, *Timothy*, 603.
[14] Mounce, *Pastoral Epistles*, 574.

designed only to entertain and divert, to make the listeners feel better about themselves.

Verse 4 The titillated ears become traitor ears, for they turn away from the truth and turn to fables. Earlier in the letter Paul had told Timothy of individuals who had proved untrue: 'all they which are in Asia be turned away from me' (1:15). The people he describes here display a similar level of inconstancy. The order in the verse is solemn. It is not that these people have been seduced from the truth by the appeal of fables. Rather, they have turned to fables because they have first turned from the truth. Truth would have preserved them – which is why Timothy must keep preaching. It was their unwillingness to tolerate sound doctrine and their pursuit of teaching that validated their own unholy desires that left them vulnerable to the appeal of fables or myths. This is emphasised by the grammar. They turned their ears from truth – an action for which they, themselves, were responsible. But Paul uses the passive voice for the second verb 'they … shall be turned' to myths. To turn from truth is to place ourselves in a position of grave danger. Once we close our ears and our hearts to the truth of God's Word, we leave ourselves exposed to the attraction of error. On three other occasions in the Pastoral Epistles, Paul speaks of myths (1 Tim. 1:4, 4:7; Tit. 1:14) and on each occasion he is stressing the empty deceitfulness of these defective and damaging teachings.

Paul outlines four downward steps that end in an intellectual, moral, and spiritual state of catastrophe where empty fables are preferred to God's truth. The path to that destination began with an attitude of impatience and intolerance towards healthful doctrine, which developed into a desire for a teaching (unworthy of the name) that entertained and amused but that never challenged or corrected. Too easily and almost unawares, we can find ourselves travelling this path and our greatest safety lies in ensuring that we give God's Word its proper place in our lives.

Verse 5 With one of the pivots so characteristic of these epistles, Paul turns from the wider context back again to Timothy, to emphasise that his life must be utterly in contrast to those of whom Paul has just been speaking. Paul emphasises this contrast by echoing the four indicative verbs of verses 3 and 4 with a list of four imperative verbs that apply to Timothy:

'Watch thou in all things' – elsewhere, this verb is translated 'be sober' (1 Thess. 5:6, 8; 1 Pet. 1:13, 4:7, 5:8), and refers to a state of alertness informed by an awareness of the Lord's return or of the ferocity of opposition. Both senses are at work in this verse – Timothy has just been reminded of the difficult circumstances of his ministry, and we are still within the confines of a charge that takes its weight, in part, from Christ's coming and kingdom (v. 1). While the word can include the idea of refraining from intoxication, it is broader in its implications than this and describes the 'mental and spiritual alertness that comes from the practice of self-control.'[15] 'In all things', or 'in all situations' (NIV), Timothy is to keep his head. This self-control stands in marked contrast to the individuals in the preceding verses who have allowed their thinking to be coloured and controlled by 'their own lusts' (v. 3).

'Endure afflictions' – Paul sounds, once again, a keynote of this epistle. In 1:8 and 2:3 he used a compound form of this verb to call for Timothy to 'join in suffering' with him. Now, as Paul is about to speak of his own departure and the conclusion of his own ministry he

---

[15] Towner, *Timothy*, 606.

stresses that the faithful execution of Timothy's charge to 'preach the word' will require him to endure affliction on his own account. Again, the contrast with the preceding verses is marked. Those who sought out teachers to tickle their ears thought that Christianity was just an intellectual diversion; Timothy was to understand that it was far more serious than that.

'Do the work of an evangelist' – The word 'evangelist' (*euangelistēs*, or 'bearer of good tidings') occurs three times in the New Testament. Besides this passage, it is used in Acts 21:8 to describe Philip and in Ephesians 4 it appears in the list of those gifts given by the risen Christ 'for the perfecting of the saints, for the work of the ministry, for the edifying of the body of Christ (Eph. 4:12). Although some commentators – primarily those who deny the Pauline authorship of this epistle and who date it to the post-apostolic period – have suggested that 'the work of an evangelist' is a reference to some sort of formal ecclesiastical office, the emphasis here is 'on the task of one ... gifted [to be an evangelist]'.[16] The fact that Paul tells Timothy to 'do the work of an evangelist' has led some interpreters to distinguish between the gift of the evangelist and the work of the evangelist and to suggest that Paul is saying something like 'do the work of an evangelist, even if evangelism is not your gift'. This is to miss Paul's point. In this passage, Paul is dealing with activity, not gift. His words are no more a comment of Timothy's giftedness (or lack of it) than they are a suggestion that there is no such thing as 'a special ability to do the work [of an evangelist]'.[17] Paul is simply ordering Timothy to get on with the task of announcing

---

[16] Mounce, *Pastoral Epistles*, 526. *Ergon*, the same word for 'work' occurs in a similar connection in 1 Timothy 3:1, where Paul describes oversight as 'a good work'. Here, too, it is activity, rather than office that is in view.

[17] Berding, *What are Spiritual Gifts?* 89, 90. Berding's treatment of this passage is characteristically tendentious.

the good tidings. The task is probably to be understood as a subset of Timothy's wider responsibility to 'preach the word' (v. 2), and to have in view the preaching of the gospel to the unsaved. This is consistent with the work of Philip the evangelist as recorded in Acts 8 and with the list of gifts given in Ephesians 4:11, where evangelists are distinct from, and complementary to the pastor teachers, whose primary responsibility is to those already saved.

'Make full proof of thy ministry' – This imperative brings Paul's charge to a close, although, in a fashion typical to this epistle, he will drive his point home in the following verses by reminding Timothy of his own example. The importance of that example will be further emphasised by his echo of the word translated 'full proof' here in verse 17, when he tells Timothy that God had strengthened him so 'that by me the preaching might be fully known'. In this verse, the verb carries the sense of discharging, completing, or finishing a task. 'In secular use the verb sometimes denotes fulfilling a promise, and even more commonly refers to the repayment of a debt (whether the obligation in view is financial or moral).'[18] The moral universe of this letter is populated with people who gave up, who diverted and deserted and departed. Led astray by error, by lust, by shame, they missed the destination for which they should have aimed. Tragically, they did not make full proof of their ministry. But Paul was cast from a different mould, for he was on the very point of finishing his course (v. 7). And it was to be his example that Timothy would emulate. His ministry, as detailed so clearly in this epistle, and even this chapter, was a comprehensive and challenging one. His responsibilities were variegated and the difficulties he faced daunting in the extreme.

[18] Towner, *Timothy*, 608.

But, for all that, he is not to be satisfied with any partial performance of his responsibilities, no mere instalments on the great debt that he owed. And though there was undoubtedly a debt that he owed to Paul, Timothy had been reminded of his most important creditors in verse 1: 'God, and the Lord Jesus Christ, who shall judge the quick and the dead'.

To say that these verses are challenging is to resort to platitude. We can only imagine how they must have searched the recesses of Timothy's soul and they should have a similar effect on all those to whom the responsibility of teaching God's Word or preaching the gospel has been given. But the impact of these words should affect every believer. None of us have precisely the commission that Timothy did, and our ministry may differ decidedly from his. But whatever our ministry may be, we are to fulfil it. We are all God's servants and serving God is a serious matter. It is not something that we can play at, no mere diversion for the dilettante. Our ministry has been given to us to fulfil, our course set before us so that we might finish it. And it is God's Word, and our appetite for and openness to its truth that will preserve us from being turned aside, stopping short, or turning back and keep us going on until, by God's grace, our debt is discharged, our mission accomplished, and our ministry fulfilled.

Verse 6 With the emphatic 'I' that begins this verse, Paul turns, as he so often does in these epistles, to his own example. Although the verses that follow are not formally part of the charge to Timothy, they are intimately related to it, for these are more than just interesting autobiographical reflections. Rather, Paul turns to his own example in order to emphasise two things. Firstly, he underlines the solemnity of the charge by making it clear to Timothy that he will, very soon, have to stand without the assistance of the apostle. The attention that Paul pays to the vital subject of transition is striking and should be a rebuke to our all too frequent failure to look beyond our own lifetime. Paul's preparation for his departure and his identification of a suitable successor were vital elements in the fulfilling of his ministry and the finishing of his course. Without them, his service would have been incomplete and, if we give no thought to how the work in which we are involved is to be carried on after we depart, our service will be incomplete too. Paul had identified a successor, but, as this epistle makes abundantly clear, he had also invested in him. That investment was a large part of the reason that he could now, with confidence, hand over to this young man a tremendous burden of responsibility. The time had now come for that transfer to take place and these verses leave Timothy in no doubt that the apostle's charge was not just important, it was immediate too. The training was over; Timothy was stepping onto the front line.

But if Paul's words emphasise the urgency of the charge and the responsibility that it brings, they also provide Timothy with motivation and reassurance. Paul's completed fight and finished course lend impetus to his command to Timothy to 'fulfil' his ministry. What he orders Timothy to do, he has himself achieved and his example is both a motivation for Timothy (and for us) and a reassuring reminder that, with God's help, it is possible to for God's servants to bring their service to a triumphant conclusion.

Paul can have harboured few illusions about the death that awaited him. Although his Roman citizenship spared him from the more barbaric forms of execution, there would be nothing glorious about the enforced march along the Ostian Way, or the execution that awaited him at his journey's end. Yet, as he speaks about that death, Paul describes it in the language of worship: 'I am now ready to be offered', to be poured out as a drink offering. Earlier in his life, Paul had used the same language in Philippians 2:17 (the only other occurrence of this word in the New Testament). There, his language had expressed uncertainty: '[even] if I be offered upon the sacrifice and service of your faith'. Here, he expresses certainty – indeed, the sacrifice is already 'an act that is underway or in progress, and therefore inevitable, though the conclusion of the act itself may be yet some distance off'.[19] What the world would see as an act of execution, Paul saw as an act of worship. And while an executioner's arm would wield the axe, Paul saw behind it all a greater power – the passive form of the verb does not identify an agent and here, as in many instances, suggests that it is God Who is acting. There was about Paul's death nothing meaningless or insignificant.

In the second half of the verse, Paul shifts metaphor: 'the time of my departure'. Although often used for death, the word has, in its origins, the idea of loosening and was used of a ship letting go its moorings or the breaking up of an encampment.[20] Here, again, there is a deliberate mismatch between the way in which Paul's death is described and what that death was actually like. His death would be violent and sudden, but he presents it here as a loosening of the bands that tie him to earth. Paul had known a good deal, in the latter part of his life, about bondage and confinement. Now he would be loosed from all the suffering and, like a boat leaving the quay, would slip gently into the element for which he

---

[19] Towner, *Timothy*, 610, hence the ESV rendering: 'I am already being poured out as a drink offering'.
[20] Thayer, *Greek Lexicon, s.v.*

had been fashioned. 'The two images [in the verse] then to some extent correspond, for the end of this life (outpoured as a libation) is the beginning of another (putting out to sea).'[21]

Verse 7 While verse 6 stresses the imminence of Paul's departure, the three staccato statements in this verse highlight the victorious nature of that departure, while continuing to hint at the operation of a Divine plan behind the actions of Paul's judges and executioners. Paul is ready to be offered because, to follow the word-order in the Greek, 'the good fight I have fought, the race I have finished, the faith I have kept'. His execution will not disrupt his service mid-stream, rather it will simply be the full stop at the end of the sentence of Paul's life, the final act of a service that has been fulfilled. His example assures Timothy that he, too, can 'fulfil his ministry' and it reminds all of us that it is possible, and should be our goal, to arrive at the end of life with our service complete, our fight fought, our race run, and with the faith safely kept.

There is some debate about the background to the first metaphor that Paul uses here. It could be military or athletic. Most commentators argue for the latter, on the basis that 'finishing the course' and winning the crown (v. 8) both unquestionably draw on the realm of

---

[21] Stott, *2 Timothy*, 113. We should, if only for completeness, note that Michael Prior, *Paul the Letter-Writer and the Second Letter to Timothy* (Sheffield: JSOT Press, 1989), Craig A. Smith, *Timothy's Task, Paul's Prospect: A New Reading of 2 Timothy*, (Sheffield: Sheffield Phoenix Press, 2006) and Craig A. Smith, *2 Timothy*, Readings: A New Biblical Commentary, (Sheffield: Sheffield Phoenix Press, 2016) argue that this verse does not speak about Paul's death but, rather, about his anticipation of an imminent release, which will allow him to continue pouring himself out in service and which will involve the literal loosing of his bonds. This thesis has not garnered much support.

athletics.²² However, against this, it must be noted that, in 2:4, 5, Paul has juxtaposed military and sporting metaphors without any sense of incongruity, and it is entirely possible that he is doing the same thing here, perhaps with a deliberate echo of chapter 2. In any case, the sense of completion and of triumph that he is conveying is clear. Paul has crossed the finishing line, leaving no last yard unrun. And he has 'kept the faith'. This could be a reference to Paul's personal faithfulness: that his confidence in Christ has never faltered through all the vicissitudes of his life and that he has discharged his apostolic calling faithfully.²³ More likely, though, in the context of this epistle and of the charge to Timothy, Paul is thinking of the precious deposit of the faith (1 Tim. 6:20; 2 Tim. 1:12; 1:14).²⁴ The faith had been entrusted to Paul, and amidst and against all who sought to adulterate or attenuate it, he had kept it, guarded it, preserved it.²⁵

Verse 8 'Henceforth' emphasises, not a chronological sequence, but a causal one. The fact that there is a crown 'laid up', 'reserved as a reward of recompense' (*BDAG*), is the direct consequence of Paul's victorious completion of his course. The crown is the *stephanos*, the crown

---

[22] In addition, some commentators have seen in 'kept the faith' a reference to 'keeping the rules of the race' (Towner, *Timothy*, 613).
[23] Fee, *1 & 2 Timothy*, Kelly, *Pastoral Epistles*, 209; and Knight III, *Pastoral Epistles*, 460. This reading does have the advantage of maintaining the consistency of the three statements in the verse.
[24] Mounce, *Pastoral Epistles*, 580 and Stott, *2 Timothy*, 114. Towner (614) argues that 'This is a case where the ambiguity of the reference to "keeping the faith" intentionally invites the wider rather than the narrower of possible readings: if the widest meaning is intended ... it must incorporate the narrower specifics.'
[25] This is the word used throughout the NT of keeping God's commandments. It is also used, in John 17:11, 12 of the keeping of believers by the Father and the Son.

awarded to the victor in the games. A 'crown of righteousness' could describe a crown consisting of righteousness – and hence Paul could be speaking of 'the moment at which the gift (symbolised by the crown) of God's righteousness is fully experienced.'[26] Or, the emphasis could be that this is a crown justly awarded to the righteous. In the context, the second meaning seems a better fit, especially in light of the description of the Lord as 'the righteous judge' and the verb that Paul uses for 'give' (*apodidōmi*), which has 'a strong sense of paying out what is due'.[27] Paul's crown, the reward that his service receives, will be righteously apportioned – he will have no basis and no need to complain that he has been unjustly treated.

The relevance of this prospect to Timothy has already been demonstrated in Paul's charge before 'the Lord Jesus Christ, who shall judge the quick and the dead' (v. 1). Paul's reference here to 'that day' likewise picks up the mention of 'His appearing and His kingdom' in verse 1, looking forward to the judgement seat of Christ and the day when service will be righteously reviewed and rewarded. This relevance is further emphasised in the verse as Paul opens the scope of the reward. There is a crown safely reserved for the apostle, but not only for him. A similar award awaits 'all them also that love His appearing'. Paul has already directed Timothy's attention to the appearing as a motive for his service (v. 1). Now, it is presented as a motive for the service of every believer. As the close connection between 'His appearing and kingdom' in verse 1 indicates, the emphasis is not on the Rapture, but rather on the manifestation of the Lord Jesus Christ. That event will vindicate every claim that Christ made about Himself

---

[26] Towner, *Timothy*, 615.
[27] Towner, *Timothy*, 614.

and will give the lie to every calumny spoken against Him during His first advent and ever since. And it will vindicate those who have been identified with Him, who have served Him and suffered for Him. It should loom large on the horizon of our lives and be the object of our love and longing.

To love His appearing is not just to have an abstract love for the concept. Rather, to love His appearing is to have our affections so focused on the Lord's return that our values, priorities, and actions will be shaped by that impending event. Lives lived like that will abound in service, in faithfulness, and in fruit, and if we live like that we can be assured that the righteous Judge will assign to us, as our deserved portion, the crown of righteousness that even now is reserved for us. As we long for His appearing may we, by His grace, fulfil our ministry, fight our fight, finish our course, and keep the faith.

4:9–21 THE ASSOCIATES OF THE MAN OF GOD

vv. 9, 10a   Disappointing Associates

Verse 9 There is no suggestion of arrogance about Paul's summary of his service in verses 6–8 of this chapter. Paul is expressing a confident and clear-eyed assessment of his service: he is not boasting or bragging. That this is so is movingly conveyed by the plea of this verse: 'Do thy diligence to come shortly unto me' and its reiteration in verse 21. Paul is no monument of self-sufficiency. In the darkness of the prison and under the shadow of impending death, he desires to have his beloved Timothy with him. Timothy is to be diligent – the same word that Paul used in 2:15. He is to let no obstacle stand in his way, for Paul wants him to come swiftly. In Titus 3:12, Paul had exhorted another servant to 'be diligent to come unto me to Nicopolis', but now the impending onset of winter and the certainty that the time of departure drew near called for added urgency – Timothy must come 'shortly'.

Verse 10 explains why Paul is so anxious for Timothy to come. The departure of a number of his co-workers and associates had left the apostle isolated. The saddest of these departures was that of Demas, which was 'of both a moral and geographical nature'.[28] The tragedy of Demas' departure was the motive that lay behind it: he 'loved this present world'. Demas should have loved Christ's appearing (v. 8), but instead this present age occupied his affections, filled his horizon, and drew him away from faithful service for and with the apostle. The man who had stood by Paul in his first imprisonment (Col. 4:14; Phlm. 1:24) now 'deserted' him (ESV), when it mattered most. Exactly how his love of the present world was expressed or why it took him to Thessalonica is not revealed. It may simply have been that the risk and opprobrium of association with a condemned criminal was too much for him to bear, or that he sought more comfortable circumstances elsewhere.[29] He may simply have been going home. But in whatever way his love of the present age drew him from the apostle it drew him too from the crown of righteousness, and left his name eternally linked with reproach on the pages of Holy Scripture.

vv. 10b–13   Diligent Associates

That there is no similar censure of Crescens or of Titus, suggests that their departure was of a different order. The work of God was going on in many places and the presence of these servants was required elsewhere –

---

[28] Towner, *Timothy*, 621.
[29] Marshall, *Pastoral Epistles*, 815; Quinn and. Wacker, *Timothy*, 808.

Crescens in Galatia (which, despite later tradition, probably means the Roman province in Asia, rather than Gaul) and Titus to Dalmatia, 'the southwest part of Illyricum – a Roman province within the larger provincial territory known as Illyricum' which had been evangelised by Paul before his arrest (Rom. 15:19).[30] Titus' name is familiar to us: he was a longtime associate and a trusted delegate of the apostle.[31] Crescens, on the other hand, is mentioned only here. Doubtless Paul felt the absence of these men keenly, and the temptation to keep them with him must have been very real. But, to imagine a Paul who would put his own personal comfort before the spread of the gospel or who would lose sight of the bigger picture in the distress of his own circumstances, we would have to disregard the clear testimony of all his writings – for Paul, the work of God came first.

Verse 11 'Only Luke is with me.' At first glance, this statement seems to be contradicted by the greetings that Paul sends in verse 21, which seem to indicate that he was in touch with a fairly sizeable number of 'brethren'. However, Paul uses the expression 'with me' with the emphatic personal pronoun when speaking of his fellow workers, those, we might say, who are a part of his team.[32] Of those fellow workers who accompanied Paul, only Luke remains. It is not difficult to appreciate God's grace in providing for His servant here – in the privations of his imprisonment Paul had the company and care of 'the beloved physician' (Col. 4:14), a man who had both the skill and the character to be of valuable help to Paul.[33]

---

[30] Towner, *Timothy*, 624.
[31] Titus's name appears eleven times outside of the pastoral epistles: 2 Cor. 2:13; 7:6, 13, 14; 8:6, 16, 23; 2 Cor. 12:18; Gal. 2:1, 3. See Hiebert, *Personalities around Paul*, 114–124.
[32] Quinn, Wacker, *Timothy*, 811.
[33] Hiebert, *Personalities*, 63–75.

The next name mentioned is another indication of Divine grace. Although it is often speculated that the 'young man' mentioned in Mark's account of Gethsemene is Mark himself, (Mk 14:51–52), his first mention by name occurs in Acts 12, where he joined Barnabas and Paul as they left Jerusalem for Antioch. There, he served the missionaries as their 'minister' or attendant (Acts 13:5). But his service was short-lived, for as Paul and his company 'came to Perga in Pamphylia: and John [Mark] departing from them, returned to Jerusalem' (Acts 13:13). The reasons behind this return from service are not told us, but Paul's reaction to Barnabas's suggestion that Mark would rejoin them at Antioch makes it clear that he regarded Mark as having failed in his responsibility during the earlier journey: 'Paul thought not good to take him with them, who departed from them from Pamphylia, and went not with them to the work' (Acts 15:38). That unwillingness to bring Mark with him resulted in 'sharp contention' between Paul and Barnabas and the sundering of what had been a happy and harmonious partnership. Such was Mark's CV – he had failed himself and caused disharmony between God's servants. Given that record, we might not have expected him to appear again on the pages of Scripture – and had we been in Paul's shoes might not have wanted him to. But Mark has been restored and he receives a warm commendation from the apostle: 'he is profitable to me for the ministry'. 'Profitable' is literally 'useful'. Paul used the same word in 2:21 to describe cleansed vessels. Mark's problem had been departure, rather than defilement, but in the hands of the God of the second chance he becomes, once again, useful to the apostle and to God. His usefulness is for 'the ministry' – Paul wanted Mark's help not just in a practical supporting role, but for his contribution to the ongoing work of the gospel in Rome.[34]

Verse 12 Paul brings his overview of the present state of the work and the workers to an end with 'Tychicus have I sent to Ephesus'. Because Timothy was at Ephesus when Paul wrote, some have thought that the past tense is an example of the 'epistolary aorist' (that is, describing events from Timothy's perspective) and that Tychicus was the courier who carried Paul's letter to Timothy.[35] That may be so, though the information in this verse would have been somewhat redundant if Tychicus had just handed Timothy the letter, and we might have expected Paul to make more overt reference to his role. Tychicus had served as Paul's messenger during his first imprisonment (Eph. 6:21, Col. 4:7) and was clearly a man upon whom Paul could rely.[36] There has been some discussion of the verb 'sent' (*apostellō*) that Paul uses here, and 'the degree to which the use of this verb should be understood as a technical reference to "sending on apostolic business", in this case as a representative or extension of Paul himself.'[37] The debate is inconclusive and, in this instance, somewhat moot. Clearly Paul had dispatched Tychicus – for what purpose is not revealed.

As is so often the case with the concluding verses of Paul's epistles, this section of the epistle provides us with a fascinating – though partial – glimpse of the work of God being carried out in the first century. Though the example of Demas sounds a note of sadness, the overall picture that these verses give us is a positive one, marked

---

[34] Hiebert, *Personalities*, 76–87. Fee argues that 'although [the phrase is] a favourite of Paul's for the ministry of the gospel ... [it] may refer to personal service. ... Perhaps a little of both is intended.' See Fee, *1 & 2 Timothy*, 294.
[35] So, Fee, *1& 2 Timothy*, 295; Knight III, *The Pastoral Epistles*, 466.
[36] Hiebert, *Personalities*, 213–222.
[37] Towner, *Timothy*, 627, *cf.* Quinn, Wacker, *Timothy*, 813–815.

by activity and harmony as these different servants, from diverse backgrounds and with very different and even difficult pasts, all work together for the spread of the gospel and the blessing of the saints. In an epistle where Paul has focused so closely on Timothy and himself, and in which Timothy has so often and so clearly been reminded of his individual responsibility, these verses are a reminder that neither of these men was a maverick. It is not always easy for us to balance a true sense of our own responsibility with an appreciation of the work carried out by other believers. These verses teach us the valuable lesson that the work of God is not carried out by sole traders but in collaboration and cooperation. And they give us, once again, an insight into the extraordinary character of the Apostle Paul. Even with death looming, he refuses to allow himself to be distracted by self-pity. Even as he anticipates his departure, his thoughts are focused on the continuation of the work. We can learn much from his example.

Verse 13 This is a poignant verse, with its glancing insight into the conditions of Paul's imprisonment. In spite of the extremity and deprivation of his circumstances, this verse contains the only reference in the letter to Paul's personal comfort. He wastes no time on self-pity, but behind the request for his cloak and the reference to the impending arrival of winter in verse 21, we can see something of the difficulties involved in his imprisonment. As temperatures fell, there would be real benefit in having his cloak with him. 'This garment was a heavy circular-shaped cape, made from goat hair, hide, or coarse wool, for outer wear. ... It was not a garment one took lightly, for it would have been relatively expensive, most men owning only one such piece of clothing, and it doubled as an outer protective covering for sleeping.'³⁸ Its value in a chilly Roman jail would be obvious. How the cloak came to be at Troas, whether Paul had left it there deliberately (as 'I left' might imply) or whether it was abandoned somehow in the turmoil of Paul's apprehension and arrest cannot be more than matter for speculation.

What is not a matter of speculation is that this request, with its practical urgency and immediacy, is a problem for those who suggest that this epistle is not authentically Pauline, for 'it is hard to believe that someone would invent material such as this.'³⁹ Moreover, 'the request seems not only abrupt but perhaps even awkward following the dramatic announcement of Paul's imminent death',⁴⁰ and while it is easy to imagine Paul refusing to dwell on that death and pressing on the practical matters, it is more difficult to imagine a forger (which, no matter how well intentioned, is what he would be) opting for this juxtaposition of the heroic and the everyday.⁴¹

Paul has interests beyond his physical comfort: he wants 'the books, but especially the parchments.'⁴² 'Books' (*biblion*) could describe either scrolls or a codices (a codex was a simple form of book, comprising of a number of leaves sewn together, and folded in half), made from papyrus. It is possible that Paul is referring here to portions of Old Testament Scripture which usually circulated in scroll (book roll) format. The second category of texts that Paul mentions –

---

³⁸ Towner, 628–629.
³⁹ Witherington III, *Letters*, (Nottingham: Apollos, 2006), 378. Fee says that it 'puts considerable strain on theories of pseudepigraphy' (Fee, *1 & 2 Timothy*, 295).
⁴⁰ Wall, *1 & 2 Timothy and Titus*, (Grand Rapids, MI: Eerdmans, 2012), 286.
⁴¹ See the discussion in Marshall, *Pastoral Epistles*, 820.
⁴² This could also be rendered 'the books, that is the parchments'. See, for a detailed discussion, T.C. Skeat, '"Especially the Parchments": A Note On 2 Timothy IV.13', *The Journal of Theological Studies*, 30:1, (1979), 173–177.

'parchments' – is intriguing. The word used here is *membrana*, a Latin loan word for texts written not on papyrus but on parchment, most likely describing parchment codices. At this point in history, the codex form was generally used for notebooks or other ephemeral texts. For important texts the scroll was still the preferred medium. But that was about to change, for early Christians displayed an overwhelming preference for the codex form for their Scriptures. Why this should have been so is one of the great perplexities of book history but one of the most plausible explanations is that an important text or collection of texts circulated widely in codex form, thus cementing the link between Scripture and codex. While some scholars have suggested that one of the gospels (probably Mark) or a collection of the four gospels might be the text most likely to have had this influence, others have suggested that a collection of Paul's epistles may be a more probable candidate. All this is rather speculative, but it is possible, perhaps even probable, that the parchments that Paul speaks of here are copies of his own epistles, the codification of what he had spoken of in 3:14 as 'the things which thou hast learned and hast been assured of'.[43]

Having said all that, it is asking too much of an author, publisher, and general bibliophile to comment on this

---

[43] See, for wider discussions of the issues raised in this paragraph, H. Roberts and T.C. Skeat, *The Birth of the Codex*, (London: Oxford University Press, 1983); Harry Y. Gamble, *Books and Readers in the Early Church: A History of Early Christian Texts*, (New Haven: Yale University Press, 1995), esp. 42–81; Eldon Jay Epp, *Perspectives on New Testament Textual Criticism: Collected Essays, 1962–2004*, Novum Testamentum, Supplements, Volume: 116, (Leiden: Brill, 2002), 521–550; and Larry W. Hurtado, *The Earliest Christian Artifacts*, (Grand Rapids, MI: Eerdmans, 2006), 43–94. Also interesting in this connection are the suggestions of David Trobisch, *Paul's Letter Collection: Tracing the Origins*, (Minneapolis: Fortress Press, 1994), though his conclusions have commanded little scholarly support and should be approached with some caution.

verse without remarking on the importance that Paul attaches to books! There could hardly be a better way to do that than by quoting from Spurgeon's sermon on this verse:

> A man who comes up into the pulpit, professes to take his text on the spot, and talks any quantity of nonsense, is the idol of many. If he will speak without premeditation, or pretend to do so, and never produce what they call a dish of dead men's brains—oh! that is the preacher. How rebuked are they by the apostle! He is inspired, and yet he wants books! He has been preaching at least for thirty years, and yet he wants books! He had seen the Lord, and yet he wants books! He had had a wider experience than most men, and yet he wants books! He had been caught up into the third heaven, and had heard things which it was unlawful for a man to utter, yet he wants books! He had written the major part of the New Testament, and yet he wants books! The apostle says to Timothy and so he says to every preacher, "Give thyself unto reading". The man who never reads will never be read; he who never quotes will never be quoted. He who will not use the thoughts of other men's brains, proves that he has no brains of his own.'[44]

To which little can be added, beyond 'amen'.

The requests of this verse have another important lesson for us. Paul, we have just seen, is facing death – he anticipates it imminently. But he does not allow that anticipation to paralyse him. 'Much like the closing of

---

[44] The full text of this sermon, which falls firmly into the category of recommended reading, can be found at
https://www.spurgeon.org/resource-library/sermons/paul-his-cloak-and-his-books.

Acts, which portrays Paul awaiting his fate by doing what he has always done (Acts 28:30, 31), here he faces death by staying in the moment, keeping warm and studying.'[45] Maintaining focus in the face of stressful circumstances is not easy for anyone and is especially difficult for some types of personality. But we would all do well to emulate Paul's example here and, while we await the outcome of events or processes that we cannot influence, simply get on with the work in hand, doing the next available thing and leaving with the Lord what we cannot control. Not only will doing so make us more profitable servants; it will make us happier Christians too.

vv. 14, 15   Damaging Associates

Paul now moves to warn Timothy of a man called 'Alexander the coppersmith'. That he is dealt with here suggests that he is not just another false teacher, and that his mention is juxtaposed with an account of Paul's 'first answer' suggests that he may have been involved somehow in Paul's re-arrest and imprisonment. Indeed, the verb translated 'did me much evil' 'may also be used in the legal sense of "to bring charges against, to accuse" which would lead to a different assessment of the syntax and the translation "[he] accused me of many evil things".'[46] Moreover, the expression 'he hath greatly withstood our words' in verse 15 could refer 'to Paul's words of defence at his trial', though over against this must be placed the fact that 'withstood' echoes the words used of the false teachers in 3:8, a circumstance which may suggest that opposition to apostolic teaching more generally is in view here also.[47] Again, we can easily

---

[45] Wall, *Timothy*, 286.
[46] Towner, *Timothy*, 631.
[47] Mounce, *Pastoral Epistles*, 593.

find ourselves verging into speculation, as we do, too, when we wonder whether this Alexander is the same as the one who got caught up in the riot at Ephesus (Acts 19:33) or – as seems likely – as the Alexander who, along with Hymenaeus, Paul 'delivered unto Satan, that [he might] learn not to blaspheme' (1 Tim. 1:20). That this Alexander is designated 'the coppersmith' (or metalworker) suggest that there was more than one Alexander known to Timothy, and whatever his link to Paul's circumstances might have been, Paul's warning suggests that Timothy was likely to encounter him – either at Ephesus or in Rome when he made his way to Paul's side.

Alexander may have had a vendetta against Paul; Paul had no such vendetta against him. However Alexander may have harmed him, he was content to leave his judgement in God's hands: 'the Lord reward him according to his works'.[48] The word 'reward' is the same as used in verse 8 of the crown that 'the Lord, the righteous judge' will award to Paul: God, who is faithful to reward His servants is faithful, too, to punish those who do 'much evil'.

Verse 15 Paul's animadversion of Alexander is not mere gossip or character assassination. Rather, the apostle mentions him as a warning to Timothy. To 'be ware' has the sense of keeping watch, and here could be translated 'be on guard against'. Alexander's opposition was not just to Paul personally – Timothy could expect him to be just as opposed to him. His opposition, whether to Paul's defence or to the message that the apostle preached, was

---

[48] A few MSS contain a form of the verb that would make this a wish or an imprecation. This is unlikely to be the correct reading: 'the variant is not strongly attested, and the future indicative creates a contrasting pattern with 4:8' (Towner, *Timothy*, 633, n.71, cf. Mounce, *Pastoral Epistles*, 593, 594). The NKJV is unusual in following this reading ('May the Lord repay him').

'great', 'exceedingly beyond measure', and Timothy could easily find himself squarely in the crosshairs of this apostate's attack.

To break off our reading at this point would give us the impression that Alexander's opposition to the apostolic words had been successful. Paul is imprisoned, and might almost think that Alexander's evil had triumphed, that the proclamation of Paul's message had been fatally stymied. But, even as Paul's requests focus our attention on the fact of his incarceration, his mention of the books and parchments hints at his continuing labour and the enduring power of the written word. But before Paul's next sentence comes to an end, these hints will have given way to a triumphant declaration of 'mission accomplished' – Paul's work was finished, not because Alexander had brought it to a premature end, but because Divine power and providence had enabled Paul to complete it.

vv. 16–18   Divine Assistance

Verse 16 'At my first answer no man stood with me'. We will need to pay some attention to the legal detail that stands behind this statement, but, interesting and important though such detail is, we must not allow it to obscure the poignancy and pathos of Paul's statement. His 'first answer' (or defence) was likely an event of considerable size. Unquestionably, it was an event of considerable consequence and thus of considerable pressure – at stake was not just deliverance 'from the mouth of the lion' but the accomplishment of Paul's mission. It was, in short, precisely the sort of moment when the friendship, fellowship, and support of the believers would have mattered most. And yet, the apostle who was owed so much by so many had stood before the panoply of Roman power alone, as far as any human help was concerned. In this, as in so many of his sufferings, he was the imitator of his Master, of Whom it was written 'they all forsook Him, and fled' (Mk 14:50). Indeed, the verb that Paul uses here to describe the way in which he has been deserted is the same as that used in the Greek translation of Psalm 22:1 and as the word 'forsaken' used by the Saviour on the cross. Nor was Paul's likeness to Christ limited to the circumstances that he experienced. It can be seen, too, in his response to those circumstances, his prayer for those who had left him to stand alone, that their failure – their betrayal – might 'not be laid to their charge'.

There has been some debate about what – and when – Paul's first answer was. The traditional view from the time of Eusebius was that Paul is referring to the juridical hearing that took place at the end of his first captivity in Rome (as recorded in Acts 28). In addition to having whatever weight we might give to tradition, this view does make good sense of Paul's deliverance from 'the mouth of the lion', for just about the only thing we can say with any confidence about that first legal process is that it resulted in Paul's release. It is, perhaps, difficult to account for Paul's sudden turn to events at such a historical remove, though it could be argued that Alexander's opposition found its expression at that time, and that the mention of his name has led Paul to recall the circumstances that flowed from the 'much evil' done by that man. Even so, it is difficult to see what Paul's purpose would be in reminding Timothy of events that he was surely already familiar with.[49] It seems more likely that Paul is speaking here about the recent events of his imprisonment, and that he is bringing Timothy up

---

[49] Though *cf.* Marshall, *Pastoral Epistles*, 825: '... people do as a matter of fact refer to things already known to their correspondents, especially when they are placing an interpretation on them.'

to date with what has been happening, not in the distant, but in the recent past.

This scenario fits well with our knowledge of Roman jurisprudence: most recent commentators have taken the 'first answer' to be the stage of the Roman legal process known as the *prima actio*, a proceeding roughly equivalent to the modern arraignment. That hearing would be followed either by a ruling that there was insufficient evidence to proceed with the case or a *secunda actio*, the trial proper. One slight issue with this view is that it slightly complicates the interpretation of Paul's deliverance from the lion's mouth but, as we shall see, that is hardly an insurmountable difficulty.

If it is true that we should not allow the niceties of the Roman legal system to blind us to the pathos of Paul's plight, it is also the case that we should not allow them to distract us from his solemn words regarding those who chose not to stand by him. His prayer (and though the words 'I pray God' have been supplied by the translators of the AV, it is, nonetheless a prayer) that their failure will not be 'laid to their charge'. 'Laid to their charge' translates *logizomai*, a verb meaning 'count up' or 'reckon', which is often used to describe 'the tallying of sins or righteous acts as personal debts or credits', and is used, in this sense, by Paul in Romans 4:11, 22.[50] The word may also play on the term for Paul's defence, *apologia* – Paul prays that God will not prefer charges against these believers on account of their failure to stand by him.

What makes this prayer so solemn is the fact that it speaks to the eternal consequences of the Christians' cowardice. It is easy to understand why they failed to stand with Paul, easy to sympathise with their unwillingness to expose themselves to pressure,

---

[50] Towner, *Timothy*, 639.

opprobrium, and even jeopardy of life and possessions. We may well feel, if we look inward, with an honest eye, that we would likely have done little better in the test. But we do well to note that their failure to stand with Paul in the moment of pressure was not only noted by the apostle; it was also noted by God. Loyalty is not easy when it is costly, and there is a natural urge to 'cut and run'. But the cost of disloyalty, Paul suggests, is even greater and longer lasting, if our failure is charged to our eternal account.

Verse 17 Paul's converts, friends, and co-workers may have failed but, as he stood before his judges, the cynosure of a hostile courtroom, Paul did not stand alone, for the Lord stood at his side. On his way to Rome the first time, Paul had known what it was for an 'angel of God' to stand by him (Acts 27:23), but in this moment of extremity, it is the Lord Who stands with him, and Who empowered him. This reference to Divine empowerment (*endynamoō*) restates one of the major themes of this epistle and directly echoes Paul's instruction to Timothy to 'be strong in the grace that is in Christ Jesus. (2:1).

The trauma and difficulty of an arraignment before a Roman court, with the very real possibility that a sentence of death would be the outcome would seem to us more than sufficient grounds for Paul to have needed God's help. But Paul, characteristically, is not thinking of himself. Rather, his focus is on the gospel and on the laying of the capstone to his life of service – the emphatic 'through me' stresses his personal responsibility for this proclamation. That Paul had proclaimed the gospel at his 'first answer' is no surprise. What is striking is the significance that he attaches to that 'proclamation'. The purpose of the Divine assistance was so that Paul might successfully execute 'an event of proclamation that for Paul was symbolic of the completion of his mission ... "the accomplishment of the proclamation through me"'.[51] The language used emphasises the significance of this event: 'accomplishment' is the word translated 'full proof' in relation to Timothy's ministry in verse 5 of this chapter.

How was the proclamation, a word that 'combines the thought of the message and its preaching, with the stress here on the activity', fulfilled?[52] This was accomplished, says Paul, by the fact that 'all the Gentiles' heard. It is likely that a large audience did attend Paul's first answer but, no matter how large it was, it could never have encompassed 'all the Gentiles'. But as the apostle to the Gentiles, whose service had taken him to the far reaches of the known world, stood before Caesar, at the heart of the Roman empire, in the world's capital, and before its highest tribunal and proclaimed, as he had so often done, the message of the gospel, he recognised that this was mission accomplished – he had finished his course and fulfilled the preaching. A moment of loneliness, of desertion, of betrayal was also a moment of triumph, accomplished, as all Paul's service had been, by the power of the God Who stood with him and strengthened him.

The God Who strengthened him also delivered him 'out of the mouth of the lion'.[53] Various suggestions have been offered about the identity of this lion and the nature of Paul's deliverance. Nero, Rome, and death have all been suggested as possibilities and, if Paul were

---

[51] Towner, *Timothy*, 642.
[52] Towner, *Timothy*, 642; Mounce, *Pastoral Epistles*, 596.
[53] The translators have supplied the article; the fact that 'lion' is anarthous in the text might discourage us from trying to pin it down to a single referent. See the discussion in Mounce, *Pastoral Epistles*, 597 and Marshall, *Pastoral Epistles*, 825.

speaking of the hearing that brought his first imprisonment to an end, any or all of these would fit. But if, as we have argued, he is speaking here of a more recent hearing that fell within his second imprisonment, then he is speaking of deliverance in a more limited sense, and, as Rome still held him firmly in her clutches, is most likely speaking about death. Paul's first hearing had resulted, not in an immediate trial, or in immediate execution, but a temporary and partial reprieve had been permitted him.

Verse 18 That partial reprieve prefigured a future and greater deliverance. Paul looks forward to a deliverance from every evil work and a saving (a better rendering of *sōzō* than the KJV's 'preserve') 'away from the sphere of evil in any form'.[54] Paul was no stranger to 'evil deeds' – Alexander was just one of the opponents who had set out to do him harm. But no matter how malevolent the design or how great the power behind it, Paul was confident in his ultimate deliverance. Rome might have held him in her grasp, but he was destined for a kingdom far greater and more powerful. Paul's place in that coming kingdom was sure, no matter what suffering he might be called upon to pass through. He has already spoken to Timothy of this kingdom, which he associated closely with Christ's appearing, in order to motivate his service (4:1) and he refers to it now to emphasise his own security.

The transition from the opening of verse 14 to the end of verse 18 is remarkable. What began with the censure of a man who had done Paul 'much evil' ends with the worship of the Lord Who will deliver him from 'every evil work'. Alexander's evil had issued in what seemed

---

[54] Charles John Ellicott, *The Pastoral Epistles of St. Paul*, 3rd ed. (London: Longman, 1864), 163.

to be the end of the road for Paul – imprisonment, desertion, death. But Paul's road would not end until he arrived safely in the heavenly kingdom and, in the meantime, God had turned its valleys into mountains. Long ago, at his conversion, God had identified Paul as 'a chosen vessel unto Me, to bear My name before the Gentiles, and kings, and the children of Israel' (Acts 9:15). Now, in the unlikely surroundings of a Roman prison, He brought His great programme for Paul's life to a triumphant conclusion. Little wonder, then, that Paul breaks out into a doxology of worship: 'to Whom be glory for ever and ever. Amen.'

Before leaving this section, we should note the parallels between these verses and Psalm 22. We have already noticed that 'all men forsook me' (v. 16) echoes the opening verse of the Psalm. A less certain echo is that between the expression 'all the Gentiles' (v. 17) and the Psalmist's references to 'all the ends of the world' and 'all the kindreds of the nations' (Ps. 22:27), which is followed by a more overt resonance between the 'mouth of the lion' of 2 Timothy 4:17 and the 'lion's mouth' of Psalm 22:21. Paul's language of rescue and deliverance also finds its echo in the Psalm: the verb that he employs in verse 17 and 18 appears three times in the Greek translation of Psalm 22 (vv. 4, 8, 20), while the verb 'save' in verse 18 also appears in Psalm 22:21. Finally, Paul's reference to the 'heavenly kingdom' (*basileia*) echoes the Psalmist's statement that 'the kingdom is the Lord's' (v. 28).[55]

These parallels are interesting, but they are not just points of literary curiosity. Rather, Paul is aligning his

---

[55] This paragraph draws on the analysis in Towner, *Timothy*, 639–648. See also the discussion in G.K. Beale and D.A. Carson (eds), *Commentary on the New Testament Use of the Old Testament*, (Grand Rapids, MI: Baker Academic, 2007), 909–913.

experience – and especially the end of his life – with that of the Lord Jesus, and demonstrating that his experience follows the template established by the Saviour. And, in the context of an epistle that calls upon Timothy to be a 'partaker of the afflictions of the gospel according to the power of God' (1:8), it sets out the template for Timothy and for all those who will follow after. In suffering, as well as in service, Timothy was called, and we are called to be imitators of Paul, even as he was of Christ (1 Cor. 11:1).

vv. 19–21 Dear Associates

Verse 19 One of the great constants of Paul's character was his appreciation for his fellow saints and fellow servants. Although he had so often been disappointed and betrayed, he never became bitter or allowed the failure of some to blind him to the value of those who were faithful. It is fitting, therefore, that very nearly the final words that we have from his pen are expressions of warm Christian fellowship that give us, as so often at the close of Paul's epistles, a precious, if fleeting, insight into the logistics of the work of God in the first century.

The names mentioned first are familiar to us both from the Acts and Paul's earlier epistles. Aquila and Priscilla are mentioned six times in the New Testament and though the references are brief, they are enough to paint for us a picture of a faithful and devoted couple, wholly committed to the work of God. 'They furnish the most beautiful example known to us in the apostolic age of the power for good that may be exerted by a husband and wife working in unison for the advancement of the Gospel.'[56] They are first mentioned in Acts 18, when Paul arrives in Corinth on his second missionary journey.

---

[56] Arthur Cushman McGiffert, *A History of Christianity in the Apostolic Age*, (New York: Charles Scribner's Sons, 1916), 428.

Aquila is identified as 'a certain Jew named Aquila, born in Pontus, lately come from Italy, with his wife Priscilla; (because that Claudius had commanded all Jews to depart from Rome)' (v. 2).

Pontus was 'a region in northeastern Asia Minor on the south shore of the Black Sea (*Pontus Euxinus*), with Galatia, Cappadocia, and Armenia bordering to the south.'[57] It had a significant population of Jews – including some of those who heard Peter speak in Jerusalem on the day of Pentecost. Like many Jews of the dispersion, Aquila had a Latin name. Priscilla's name, too, is Latin, and there has been speculation that the way in which Luke introduces them in Acts 18 suggests that she may not have been a Jew. Aquila had moved from Pontus to Rome, and then, under the compulsion of the Imperial decree, to Corinth. The upheaval of this latter move must have been considerable, and it may well have seemed like a disaster to Aquila and Priscilla. But, behind the decree of Claudius was a greater and wiser hand, and this faithful couple was being moved into position so that when Paul, a fellow tentmaker, arrived in Corinth, they were able to provide him with accommodation and employment. When Paul left Corinth they travelled with him to Ephesus, remaining there when Paul moved on. It was in Ephesus that they encountered the Alexandrine Jew, Apollos, 'an eloquent man, and mighty in the scriptures' and graciously addressed his imperfect knowledge: 'they took him unto them, and expounded unto him the way of God more perfectly' (Acts 18:24, 26). In Ephesus their home provided a meeting place for a local church (1 Cor. 16:19). From there, they moved to Rome where, once again, they provided accommodation for a church (Rom. 16:3,4).

---

[57] David Noel Freedman (ed.), *Eerdmans Dictionary of the Bible*, (Grand Rapids, MI: Eerdmans, 2000), 'Aquila', *s.v.*

Now, they are back in Ephesus where they must have been an enormous help and encouragement to Timothy.

Unusually for the culture in which they lived and in contrast with Paul's references to other couples, Priscilla's name is mentioned first here and in Romans 16:3, as well as in Acts 18:18. While it is possible that this may indicate that Priscilla is of a higher social rank (and there has been some speculation to that effect) it is perhaps more likely that the order reveals something about her greater commitment and ability. However exactly the dynamics of their relationship worked, Priscilla and Aquila stand out on the pages of Scripture as an example of a diligent couple, whose home, possessions, and lives were always available for God to use and whose commitment to the apostle Paul makes them a delightful counterpoint to those who, in one way or another, turned away from them.

Having greeted a couple, Paul now greets a household. We have already encountered Onesiphorus in the epistle. 1:18 indicates that he had been of extensive help to the apostle while he was in Ephesus and, arriving in Rome, he had diligently and urgently sought out Paul and had refreshed the apostle without any thought of his own wellbeing or shame at the apostle's chain (1:16–18). It may well be that his business required his presence in Rome, but 'being in Rome, his love compelled him to look Paul up'.[58] By the time Paul writes, Onesiphorus had left Rome, but the fact that his household is greeted here seems to suggest that he has not returned home to Ephesus. Beyond that, though, this juxtaposition of a couple and a household reminds us of the importance of the domestic sphere to the work of God. We have seen already in this epistle how Timothy's home and the upbringing he received in it had played a vital role in

---

[58] Hiebert, *Personalities around Paul*, 186.

equipping him for his future service. Now, at the end of the epistle the importance, not just of individuals, but of couples and households is emphasised afresh. The conditions of twenty-first century testimony have done nothing to diminish that importance – we still need Priscillas and Aquilas and faithful and committed couples, families, and households.

Verse 20 From greetings, Paul turns to a brief update about two individuals. This is the third occurrence of the name Erastus in the New Testament. Whether this man is the same as 'Erastus the chamberlain of the city' (Rom. 16:23) whose greetings Paul sent from Corinth and how he relates to the Erastus mentioned in Acts 19:22 is unclear.[59]

Trophimus was a Gentile from the Roman province of Asia (Acts 20:4). He accompanied Paul to Macedonia in the immediate aftermath of the Ephesian riot. Later, his presence with Paul in Jerusalem caused the Jews to leap to unwarranted conclusions and was the catalyst for Paul's arrest and imprisonment. Paul says 'Trophimus have I left at Miletum sick'. This could mean that Paul and Trophimus were both at Miletus and that Paul moved on while Trophimus was left behind. Alternatively, the verb used could mean 'to assign' (as it may do in Titus 1:5), and so Paul could be saying that Trophimus became sick during his assignment in Miletus. The former possibility is more likely, and given that Miletus was close to Ephesus, where Timothy was based, Paul's mention of this detail may have been intended to serve as an encouragement for Timothy to visit Trophimus on his way to Rome. It also absolves

---

[59] Erastus' name appears on the 'Erastus inscription', discovered in Corinth in 1929. It describes him as '*aedile*' (an official responsible for the maintenance of public buildings) and commemorates his funding of a pavement.

Trophimus of any blame for not being with Paul in Rome at his moment of greatest need.

Verse 21 'Do thy diligence to come before winter.' The apostle's plea – or, rather, command – echoes the words of 4:9, but the substitution of 'before winter' for 'shortly' adds a definite timeframe. Paul had requested Timothy to bring his cloak (v. 13) and he would need the protection of that garment before the rigours of winter set in. In addition, travel during winter, especially by sea, was hazardous, and if Timothy had not made the trip before winter set in, there was little chance of his being with Paul until the spring, which might well have been too late. The words still resound with pathos; it is difficult to imagine the effect that they had on Timothy.

Paul has already sent greetings on his own behalf. Now, he adds greetings from others in Rome. As we have seen, the presence of these brethren must modify any impression that Paul was totally alone, but the fact that the names mentioned here are found only here in the New Testament and Paul's use of the catchall phrase 'all the brethren' indicate that these men are local believers with whom Paul has had contact, rather than members of what we might loosely term his 'team'.

Verse 22 It is fitting that the last recorded words of the apostle who was used of God to bring so much blessing to so many should be words of benediction and prayer. There is a prayer specifically for Timothy: 'The Lord Jesus Christ be with thy spirit' and a wider benediction: 'Grace be with you'. Most versions render the first prayer 'the Lord be with your spirit', and the manuscript support for that reading suggests that Paul did use the shorter form, with its rich Old Testament resonances. The KJV's amplification is hardly a distortion, however –

Paul's final, climactic, and crowning desire for Timothy is that, amidst all the difficulties, beneath the crushing weight of responsibility, the Lord Who Paul knew and served so well would be with his spirit. And for the others who read the letter Paul had another wish that summed up one of the chief preoccupations of his ministry and teaching: 'Grace be with you, Amen'.

With those words, silence falls on the Scriptural record of the apostle's life. We do not know whether Timothy arrived before winter, or in time to say his final goodbye to the apostle. Of Paul's last days and his final steps to the place of execution we are told nothing. But how we thank God for the ministry of that extraordinary man and for his contribution to inspired Scripture – not least for this precious epistle.

Bibliography

BAKER, J.R. *What the Bible Teaches: II Timothy.* Kilmarnock: John Ritchie Ltd, 1983.
BARRETT, C.K. *The Pastoral Epistles in the New English Bible.* Oxford: Clarendon, 1963.
BEALE, G.K. and D.A. Carson (eds), *Commentary on the New Testament Use of the Old Testament.* Grand Rapids, MI: Baker Academic, 2007.
BERDING, Kenneth. *What are Spiritual Gifts? Rethinking the Conventional View.* Grand Rapids, MI: Kregel, 2006.
BERNARD, J.H. *The Pastoral Epistles.* Cambridge: Cambridge University Press, 1906.
CAMPBELL, R. Alastair. 'Identifying the Faithful Sayings in the Pastoral Epistles'. *Journal for the Study of the New Testament,* 54 (1994), 73–86.
CARSON, D.A. *Exegetical Fallacies* (2nd ed.). Carlisle: Paternoster, 1996.
COUSER, Gregory A. '"How Firm a Foundation": The Ecclesiology of 2 Timothy 2:19–21'. *Bibliotheca Sacra,* 173, 460–475.
DIBELIUS, Martin and Hans Conzelmann. *The Pastoral Epistles.* Minneapolis, MN: Fortress Press, 1972.
ELLICOTT, Charles John. *The Pastoral Epistles of St. Paul,* 3rd ed. London: Longman, 1864.
ELLIS, James J. *Dan Crawford of Luanza.* Kilmarnock: John Ritchie, n.d.
EPP, Eldon Jay *Perspectives on New Testament Textual Criticism: Collected Essays, 1962–2004.* Novum

Testamentum, Supplements, Volume: 116. Leiden: Brill, 2002.

EUSEBIUS of Caesarea. *Eusebius' Ecclesiastical History*. Trans. C.F. Cruse. Peabody, MA: Hendrickson, 1998.

FEE, Gordon D. *1 & 2 Timothy, Titus*. Understanding the Bible Commentary Series. Grand Rapids, MI: Baker Books, 1988.

FREEDMAN, David Noel (ed.). *Eerdmans Dictionary of the Bible*. Grand Rapids, MI: Eerdmans, 2000.

FREND, W. H. C. 'Persecutions: Genesis and legacy', in M. M. Mitchell and F. M. Young (eds), *The Cambridge History of Christianity, 1: Origins to Constantine*, (Cambridge: Cambridge University Press, 2006), 503–523.

GAMBLE, Harry Y. *Books and Readers in the Early Church: A History of Early Christian Texts*. New Haven: Yale University Press, 1995.

HARRIS, Murray J. *Prepositions and Theology in the Greek New Testament*. Grand Rapids, MI: Zondervan, 2012.

HENDRIKSEN, W. *I–II Timothy and Titus*. New Testament Commentary. Grand Rapids, MI: Baker, 1957.

HIEBERT, D. Edmond. *Personalities Around Paul*. Chicago: Moody Press, 1973.

HURTADO, Larry W. *The Earliest Christian Artifacts*. Grand Rapids, MI: Eerdmans, 2006.

ICE, Thomas. 'Are We Living in the Last Days?' (2009), https://digitalcommons.liberty.edu/pretrib_arch/61/.

JOHNSON, Luke Timothy. *Letters to Paul's Delegates: 1 Timothy, 2 Timothy, Titus*. The New Testament in Context. Harrisburg, PA: Trinity Press International, 1996.

KELLY, J.N.D. *A Commentary on the Pastoral Epistles.* London: A. & C. Black, 1963.

KELLY, William. *An Exposition of the Two Epistles to Timothy* (3rd ed.). London: C.A. Hammond, 1948.

KNIGHT III, George W. *The Pastoral Epistles.* New International Greek Testament Commentary. Grand Rapids, MI: Eerdmans, 1992.

LOCK, Walter. *The Pastoral Epistles.* International Critical Commentary. Edinburgh: T&T Clark, 1924.

MACDONALD, William. *One Day at a Time: Truths to Live By.* Everyday Publications, 1985.

MARSHALL, I. Howard. *The Pastoral Epistles.* International Critical Commentary. Edinburgh: T&T Clark, 1999.

MCCORMICK, Michael. 'The Birth of the Codex and the Apostolic Life-Style', *Scriptorium*, 39:1, (1985), 150–158.

MCGIFFERT, Arthur Cushman. *A History of Christianity in the Apostolic Age.* New York: Charles Scribner's Sons, 1916.

METZGER, Bruce M. *A Textual Commentary on the Greek New Testament* (2nd ed.). Stuttgart: Deutsche Bibel Gesellschaft, 1994.

MOUNCE, William D. *Pastoral Epistles.* Word Biblical Commentary. Nashville: Thomas Nelson Publishers, 2000.

O'BRIEN, Peter. *Introductory Thanksgivings in the Letters of Paul.* Eugene, OR: Wipf and Stock, 2009.

PRIOR, Michael. *Paul the Letter-Writer and the Second Letter to Timothy.* Sheffield: JSOT Press, 1989.

QUINN, Jerome D. and William C. Wacker. *The First and Second Letters to Timothy: A New Translation with Notes and Commentary.* Grand Rapids, MI: Eerdmans 2000.

ROBERTS, H. and T.C. Skeat. *The Birth of the Codex*. London: Oxford University Press, 1983.

SHAW, Brent D. 'The Myth of the Neronian Persecution', *The Journal of Roman Studies*, 105 (2015), 73–100,

SMITH, Craig A. *2 Timothy. Readings: A New Biblical Commentary*. Sheffield: Sheffield Phoenix Press, 2016.

SMITH, Craig A. *Timothy's Task, Paul's Prospect: A New Reading of 2 Timothy*. Sheffield: Sheffield Phoenix Press, 2006.

SPICQ, Ceslas. *Theological Lexicon of the New Testament* (trans. James D. Ernest). Peabody, MA: Hendrickson, 1995.

STOTT, John. *The Bible Speaks Today: The Message of 2 Timothy*. Nottingham: Inter-Varsity Press, 1999.

SWEETNAM, Mark. 'Truth in the Pastoral Epistles (5)'. *Truth & Tidings*, (Dec, 2017). http://truthandtidings.com/2017/12/truth-in-the-pastoral-epistles-5-its-revelation-3/.

SWEETNAM, Mark. *To the Day of Eternity: Future Events in Bible Prophecy*. Lisburn: Scripture Teaching Library, 2014.

SWEETNAM, Mark. *Worship: The Christian's Highest Calling*. Lisburn: Scripture Teaching Library, 2013.

THAYER, Joseph Henry. *Thayer's Greek Lexicon of the New Testament*. Grand Rapids : Baker Book House, 1977.

TOWNER, Philip H. *The Letters to Timothy and Titus*. The New International Commentary on the New Testament. Grand Rapid, MI: Eerdmans, 2006.

TROBISCH, David. *Paul's Letter Collection: Tracing the Origins*. Minneapolis: Fortress Press, 1994.

UNGER, Merrill F. *The New Unger's Bible Dictionary*. Ed. R.K. Harrison. Chicago: Moody Press, 1988.

VAN NES, Jermo. *Pauline Language and the Pastoral Epistles: A Study of Linguistic Variation in the Corpus Paulinum.* Leiden: Brill, 2017.

VINE, W.E. *The Collected Writings of W.E. Vine (Vol. 3).* Nashville, TN: Thomas Nelson, 1996.

VINE, W.E. *Vine's Expository Dictionary of New Testament Words.* London: Oliphants, 1963.

WALL, Robert B. *1 & 2 Timothy and Titus.* The Two Horizons New Testament Commentary. Grand Rapids, MI: Eerdmans, 2012.

WARFIELD, B.B. *The Inspiration and Authority of the Bible.* London: Marshall, Morgan, and Scott Ltd, 1951.

WITHERINGTON III, Ben. *Letters and Homilies for Hellenized Christians (Vol. 1).* Nottingham: Apollos, 2006.

YARBROUGH, Robert W. *The Letters to Timothy and Titus.* The Pillar Bible Commentary. London: Apollos, 2018.

ZEHR, Paul M. *1 & 2 Timothy, Titus.* Believers Church Bible Commentary. Scottdale, PA: Herald Press, 2010.

www.ingramcontent.com/pod-product-compliance
Lightning Source LLC
Chambersburg PA
CBHW060608230426
43670CB00011B/2021